JEREM
BIBLE STUDY SERIES

LUKE

THE COMPASSION OF CHRIST

DR. DAVID JEREMIAH

Prepared by Hudson Bible

THOMAS NELSON
Since 1798

Luke
Jeremiah Bible Study Series

© 2019 by Dr. David Jeremiah

Published in Nashville, Tennessee, by Thomas Nelson. Thomas Nelson is a registered trademark of HarperCollins Christian Publishing, Inc.

Produced with the assistance of Hudson Bible (www.HudsonBible.com). Project staff include Christopher D. Hudson and Randy Southern.

All Scripture quotations, unless otherwise indicated, are taken from The Holy Bible, New King James Version. Copyright © 1979, 1980, 1982 by Thomas Nelson. All rights reserved.

The quote by Irenaeus in the Introduction is from *Against Heresies*, 3:1. The quote by Origen is from Eusebius, *History of the Church*, 6:25.

Thomas Nelson titles may be purchased in bulk for educational, business, fundraising, or sales promotional use. For information, please e-mail SpecialMarkets@ThomasNelson.com.

ISBN 978-0-310-09153-0

Second Printing July 2020 / Printed in the United States of America

CONTENTS

INTRODUCTION TO
The Gospel of Luke

"It seemed good to me also, having had perfect understanding of all things from the very first, to write to you an orderly account" (Luke 1:3). According to the apostle Paul, Luke was a "beloved physician" (Colossians 4:14) who accompanied him on several of his missionary journeys. However, Luke's real passion was in setting down an orderly account that detailed the birth, ministry, death, and resurrection of Jesus. This was a task for which Luke was well suited, for he was both a thoughtful man of science and a great observer of people. Luke thus took great care in relating the information he collected, but he also emphasized the care that Jesus, as the Great Physician, extended to people everywhere—both Jewish and Gentile alike.

AUTHOR AND DATE

The Gospel of Luke, as with the other three Gospels, does not list the name of its author. However, the earliest church fathers to mention the Gospel all concurred it was written by Luke, a second-generation follower of Christ who—as a doctor and associate of Paul—was in a position to investigate the stories about Jesus. Irenaeus, who lived c. AD 130–202, stated, "Luke . . . the companion of Paul, recorded in a book the Gospel preached by him." Origen (c. AD 185–254) noted, "The third [Gospel was written] by Luke, the Gospel commended by Paul, and composed for Gentile converts." In addition to this evidence, the writer uses specific medical terminology throughout the Gospel to describe the conditions of those who approached Jesus for healing, which lends support to the idea he had a medical background. It is likely that Luke was the last Synoptic Gospel to be written, sometime around AD 70, from the city of Rome.

BACKGROUND AND SETTING

Luke states at the beginning of his Gospel that he created his account for a person named Theophilus, whose name means "loved by God." It is possible this refers to a wealthy and influential man who, according to second-century references, lived in the city of Antioch during the time of Luke. Another possibility is that Theophilus was a general title for those across the world who had chosen to follow Christ. Either way, it is clear Luke intended his Gospel to be read by *all people*. This is evidenced by the fact that even though he included many references to Jewish practices in Israel, he also focused on Jesus' ministry to those in the Gentile world. Furthermore, Luke's genealogy of Jesus traces Christ's lineage not just to Abraham, the father of the Jewish people, but all the way back to Adam, the father of all peoples.

KEY THEMES

Several key themes are prominent in Luke's Gospel. The first is that *Jesus came with a message of salvation for all of humanity.* Luke relates that when Jesus returned to His hometown of Nazareth to begin His public ministry, He read from the prophet Isaiah and announced, "Today this Scripture is fulfilled in your hearing" (4:21). In response, the people from His own village tried to end His life by throwing Him over a cliff. The story reflects Luke's intent to show how Jesus *first* brought the good news of salvation to the Jewish people (who rejected it) and *then* to the entire world.

A second theme is that *Jesus had a heart for the marginalized in society.* When Jesus began His ministry in Nazareth, He also announced He had come to heal the sick and the brokenhearted and "set at liberty those who are oppressed" (4:18). Luke emphasizes in both Jesus' teachings and miracles that He was concerned about those on the fringe of society—whether they were despised tax collectors, widows in need, poor shepherds, or even sons in open rebellion toward God. Every person was important to Jesus and a candidate for salvation.

A third theme is that *Jesus operated through the power of the Holy Spirit.* Luke reports that Jesus was conceived by the Holy Spirit and, after His baptism (where the Holy Spirit descended over Him like a dove), was led into the wilderness by the Holy Spirit to be tempted. Jesus announced at the beginning of His ministry that "the Spirit of the LORD" was upon Him (4:18). Later, after Jesus' resurrection, He told His disciples they could receive that same power and instructed them to wait in Jerusalem for the coming of the Holy Spirit (see 24:49).

A fourth theme is that *Jesus was fully divine but also fully human.* Luke refers twenty-five times to Jesus as the "Son of Man," which is more than any other Gospel writer. His account of Jesus' life begins in the most humble of situations—a manger surrounded by animals and lowly shepherds. Yet Luke also demonstrates that Jesus knew (even from an early age) that He was the divine Son of God who had come into the world to fulfill His heavenly Father's plan of salvation. Luke's Gospel is also unique in that it concludes with Jesus being taken up to heaven, where He is seated at the right hand of God (see Luke 24:51; Acts 7:56).

KEY APPLICATIONS

Luke shows how Jesus came into this world "to *seek and to save* that which was lost" (19:10). He shows the high value Jesus places on rescuing *all people* from their sins—no matter how "far gone" those people might seem. And he shows how Jesus was willing to *give up His place in heaven* to come down to earth as a *sacrifice* for the sins of every person who will receive Him.

GOD WITH US

Luke 1:1–2:52

GETTING STARTED

If you could ask one question of Mary, the mother of Jesus, what would it be?

_____

_____

_____

_____

_____

_____

_____

_____

_____

_____

_____

_____

SETTING THE STAGE

For thousands of years, humankind gazed at God. Glimpses of His majesty would occasionally shine through, flashing forth in the handiwork of His firmament. But the fullness of His glory was too sublime for human eyes. But then, Jesus came into the world to reveal the Father in heaven. Jesus was

God manifest in the flesh. God became human to tell us what He is like. God the Son became flesh to reveal God the Father. Christ is the image of God's person.

When you look at Jesus—when you see Him healing the sick and read of His compassion for the hungry, His concern for little children, His dealings with those who are demon-possessed, His flashing anger against hypocrisy, and His pardon for sinners—then you see God and understand what God is like.

You also get a sense of what God values by how He works through the people He chose to be a part of His salvation plan. For instance, in the opening chapters of Luke's Gospel, we meet an elderly couple, Zacharias and Elizabeth, who had long ago given up hope of ever having a child. We meet Mary, an unmarried young woman from a village that was belittled by most people. We also encounter Joseph, a simple carpenter from the same village.

Even the most astute students of the Law and Prophets could not have imagined that the Messianic prophecies would be fulfilled through people like *them*. Yet God saw something in them that no one else saw. He saw an obedient spirit and a willingness to sacrifice their own desires for something far greater.

EXPLORING THE TEXT

John the Baptist's Birth Is Announced (Luke 1:5–25)

---

5 There was in the days of Herod, the king of Judea, a certain priest named Zacharias, of the division of Abijah. His wife was of the daughters of Aaron, and her name was Elizabeth. 6 And they were both righteous before God, walking in all the commandments and ordinances of the Lord blameless. 7 But they had no child, because Elizabeth was barren, and they were both well advanced in years.

8 So it was, that while he was serving as priest before God in the order of his division, 9 according to the custom of the priesthood,

his lot fell to burn incense when he went into the temple of the Lord. ¹⁰ And the whole multitude of the people was praying outside at the hour of incense. ¹¹ Then an angel of the Lord appeared to him, standing on the right side of the altar of incense. ¹² And when Zacharias saw him, he was troubled, and fear fell upon him.

¹³ But the angel said to him, "Do not be afraid, Zacharias, for your prayer is heard; and your wife Elizabeth will bear you a son, and you shall call his name John. ¹⁴ And you will have joy and gladness, and many will rejoice at his birth. ¹⁵ For he will be great in the sight of the Lord, and shall drink neither wine nor strong drink. He will also be filled with the Holy Spirit, even from his mother's womb. ¹⁶ And he will turn many of the children of Israel to the Lord their God. ¹⁷ He will also go before Him in the spirit and power of Elijah, 'to turn the hearts of the fathers to the children,' and the disobedient to the wisdom of the just, to make ready a people prepared for the Lord."

¹⁸ And Zacharias said to the angel, "How shall I know this? For I am an old man, and my wife is well advanced in years."

¹⁹ And the angel answered and said to him, "I am Gabriel, who stands in the presence of God, and was sent to speak to you and bring you these glad tidings. ²⁰ But behold, you will be mute and not able to speak until the day these things take place, because you did not believe my words which will be fulfilled in their own time."

²¹ And the people waited for Zacharias, and marveled that he lingered so long in the temple. ²² But when he came out, he could not speak to them; and they perceived that he had seen a vision in the temple, for he beckoned to them and remained speechless.

²³ So it was, as soon as the days of his service were completed, that he departed to his own house. ²⁴ Now after those days his wife Elizabeth conceived; and she hid herself five months, saying, ²⁵ "Thus the Lord has dealt with me, in the days when He looked on me, to take away my reproach among people."

1. According to the angel, what would be the role of John, the son of Zacharias and Elizabeth (see verses 13–17)?

_____

_____

_____

_____

_____

2. What caused Zacharias to be struck mute? Why did God take this action (see verses 18–20)?

_____

_____

_____

_____

_____

Jesus' Birth Is Announced (Luke 1:26–45)

²⁶ Now in the sixth month the angel Gabriel was sent by God to a city of Galilee named Nazareth, ²⁷ to a virgin betrothed to a man whose name was Joseph, of the house of David. The virgin's name was Mary. ²⁸ And having come in, the angel said to her, "Rejoice, highly favored one, the Lord is with you; blessed are you among women!"

²⁹ But when she saw him, she was troubled at his saying, and considered what manner of greeting this was. ³⁰ Then the angel said to her, "Do not be afraid, Mary, for you have found favor with God. ³¹ And behold, you will conceive in your womb and bring forth a Son, and shall call His name Jesus. ³² He will be great, and will be called the Son of the Highest; and the Lord God will give Him the throne of His father David. ³³ And He will reign over the house of Jacob forever, and of His kingdom there will be no end."

³⁴ Then Mary said to the angel, "How can this be, since I do not know a man?"

³⁵ And the angel answered and said to her, "The Holy Spirit will come upon you, and the power of the Highest will overshadow you; therefore, also, that Holy One who is to be born will be called the Son of God. ³⁶ Now indeed, Elizabeth your relative has also conceived a son in her old age; and this is now the sixth month for her who was called barren. ³⁷ For with God nothing will be impossible."

³⁸ Then Mary said, "Behold the maidservant of the Lord! Let it be to me according to your word." And the angel departed from her.

³⁹ Now Mary arose in those days and went into the hill country with haste, to a city of Judah, ⁴⁰ and entered the house of Zacharias and greeted Elizabeth. ⁴¹ And it happened, when Elizabeth heard the greeting of Mary, that the babe leaped in her womb; and Elizabeth was filled with the Holy Spirit. ⁴² Then she spoke out with a loud voice and said, "Blessed are you among women, and blessed is the fruit of your womb! ⁴³ But why is this granted to me, that the mother of my Lord should come to me? ⁴⁴ For indeed, as soon as the voice of your greeting sounded in my ears, the babe leaped in my womb for joy. ⁴⁵ Blessed is she who believed, for there will be a fulfillment of those things which were told her from the Lord."

---

3. Virtually every Jewish woman longed to give birth to the Messiah. This honor was bestowed on Mary, an unmarried teenage girl from Nazareth. Most of what we know about Mary is found in this passage. What clues do you find that help explain why God chose her?

_____

_____

_____

_____

_____

4. How did Mary respond when she received the news from Gabriel that she would give birth to the Messiah (see verses 34, 38)? How was her reaction different from Zacharias's?

_____

_____

_____

_____

The Birth of Jesus (Luke 2:1–20)

¹ And it came to pass in those days that a decree went out from Caesar Augustus that all the world should be registered. ² This census first took place while Quirinius was governing Syria. ³ So all went to be registered, everyone to his own city.

⁴ Joseph also went up from Galilee, out of the city of Nazareth, into Judea, to the city of David, which is called Bethlehem, because he was of the house and lineage of David, ⁵ to be registered with Mary, his betrothed wife, who was with child. ⁶ So it was, that while they were there, the days were completed for her to be delivered. ⁷ And she brought forth her firstborn Son, and wrapped Him in swaddling cloths, and laid Him in a manger, because there was no room for them in the inn.

⁸ Now there were in the same country shepherds living out in the fields, keeping watch over their flock by night. ⁹ And behold, an angel of the Lord stood before them, and the glory of the Lord shone around them, and they were greatly afraid. ¹⁰ Then the angel said to them, "Do not be afraid, for behold, I bring you good tidings of great joy which will be to all people. ¹¹ For there is born to you this day in the city of David a Savior, who is Christ the Lord. ¹² And this will be the sign to you: You will find a Babe wrapped in swaddling cloths, lying in a manger."

¹³ And suddenly there was with the angel a multitude of the heavenly host praising God and saying:

¹⁴ "Glory to God in the highest,
And on earth peace, goodwill toward men!"

¹⁵ So it was, when the angels had gone away from them into heaven, that the shepherds said to one another, "Let us now go to Bethlehem and see this thing that has come to pass, which the Lord has made known to us." ¹⁶ And they came with haste and found Mary and Joseph, and the Babe lying in a manger. ¹⁷ Now when they had seen Him, they made widely known the saying which was told them concerning this Child. ¹⁸ And all those who heard it marveled at those things which were told them by the shepherds. ¹⁹ But Mary kept all these things and pondered them in her heart. ²⁰ Then the shepherds returned, glorifying and praising God for all the things that they had heard and seen, as it was told them.

---

5. Micah prophesied the Messiah would be born in Bethlehem (see 5:2). What events had to occur for this to take place (see Luke 2:1–4)?

_____

_____

_____

_____

6. In first-century Israel, shepherds were generally considered lower class, and they represented the poor and humble. Given this, why do you think God chose a group of shepherds to be the first witnesses to the birth of Christ (see verses 8–16)?

_____

_____

_____

_____

Jesus Is Presented in the Temple (Luke 2:25–40)

[25] And behold, there was a man in Jerusalem whose name was Simeon, and this man was just and devout, waiting for the Consolation of Israel, and the Holy Spirit was upon him. [26] And it had been revealed to him by the Holy Spirit that he would not see death before he had seen the Lord's Christ. [27] So he came by the Spirit into the temple. And when the parents brought in the Child Jesus, to do for Him according to the custom of the law, [28] he took Him up in his arms and blessed God and said:

> [29] "Lord, now You are letting Your servant depart in peace,
> According to Your word;
> [30] For my eyes have seen Your salvation
> [31] Which You have prepared before the face of all peoples,
> [32] A light to bring revelation to the Gentiles,
> And the glory of Your people Israel."

[33] And Joseph and His mother marveled at those things which were spoken of Him. [34] Then Simeon blessed them, and said to Mary His mother, "Behold, this Child is destined for the fall and rising of many in Israel, and for a sign which will be spoken against [35] (yes, a sword will pierce through your own soul also), that the thoughts of many hearts may be revealed."

[36] Now there was one, Anna, a prophetess, the daughter of Phanuel, of the tribe of Asher. She was of a great age, and had lived with a husband seven years from her virginity; [37] and this woman was a widow of about eighty-four years, who did not depart from the temple, but served God with fastings and prayers night and day. [38] And coming in that instant she gave thanks to the Lord, and spoke of Him to all those who looked for redemption in Jerusalem.

[39] So when they had performed all things according to the law of the Lord, they returned to Galilee, to their own city, Nazareth. [40] And

the Child grew and became strong in spirit, filled with wisdom; and the grace of God was upon Him.

---

7. How does Luke describe Simeon (see verses 25–32)? How did Mary and Joseph react to Simeon's words when he encountered Jesus (see verse 33)?

_____

_____

_____

_____

8. Anna was a prophetess who likely lived in one of the rooms surrounding the temple. Why do you think Luke includes this story of her encounter with Jesus (see verses 36–38)?

_____

_____

_____

_____

REVIEWING THE STORY

According to Luke's Gospel, Mary kept the extraordinary events surrounding Jesus' birth and childhood "in her heart" (2:19, 51). Scholars believe that when Luke was gathering information for his Gospel, he turned to Mary as a source. At long last, Jesus' mother had an opportunity to share her experience with the world, and the result is the most complete version of the Advent story ever recorded. In Luke's opening chapters, he takes readers through everything from angelic visits to the miraculous pregnancies of Elizabeth and Mary, and from the events that led to Jesus' birth in Bethlehem to His earliest visits to the temple.

9. How did the angel Gabriel announce the birth of John the Baptist to Zacharias (see Luke 1:8–12)? Why did Zacharias find this impossible to believe (see verse 18)?

_____

_____

_____

_____

_____

10. How do you think Mary's time with Elizabeth prepared her for the role she would fulfill in God's plan (see Luke 1:39–45)?

_____

_____

_____

_____

_____

11. Jesus is the "King of kings and Lord of lords" (Revelation 19:16), yet it is hard to conceive of a more lowly and humble birth into the world (see Luke 2:4–7). Why do you think God chose to orchestrate the events surrounding Jesus' birth in this way?

_____

_____

_____

_____

_____

12. What prophecy did Simeon give about Jesus in the temple (see Luke 2:34–35)?

_____

_____

_____

_____

Applying the Message

13. God used an angel to communicate His will to Zacharias, Mary, and Joseph. What are some means that God uses to communicate His will to you?

_____

_____

_____

_____

14. God rewarded the faithfulness of Simeon and Anna by allowing them to see the Messiah before they died. Aside from eternal life, what would be the most meaningful way that God could reward you for your faithful service?

_____

_____

_____

Reflecting on the Meaning

How did Mary respond to the news that God was getting ready to use her in an extraordinary way? Her first reaction was *confusion*. She likely had never seen an angel before . . . nor had ever expected to see one. His appearance was so out of the ordinary, so unbelievable to her, that her mind had trouble processing it.

Mary's second reaction was *consideration*. Luke writes that she "considered what manner of greeting this was" (1:29). She mentally played back what she had heard in the angel's words, searching them for meaning.

Her third reaction was *investigation*. After considering the matter, she posed a question to the angel who had announced that she was going to give birth: "How can this be, since I do not know a man?" (verse 34). Mary had every right to question what the angel had said, because this had never happened before. Never had God created a body in a woman without the involvement of a man.

God accommodated Mary's questions. He gave Mary a miraculous precedent to which to cling. The angel revealed to Mary that her cousin Elizabeth, who had been barren her entire life and was well past her childbearing years, was also pregnant. Mary rushed to Elizabeth's house to confirm the news. She knew that if what the angel had said about Elizabeth was true, then certainly what he had said to her was also true.

This led to Mary's fourth reaction: *submission*. After visiting Elizabeth to confirm the angel's announcement, she likely wrestled with how to explain the situation to Joseph. Yet while she had few answers, she still humbly submitted to God's will. Mary also set an example for us to follow when we are confused or overwhelmed by the plan that God has laid out for us.

JOURNALING YOUR RESPONSE

How would you respond if you received an unmistakable call from God to do something extraordinary—something way outside of your comfort zone?

BAPTISM AND TEMPTATION

Luke 3:1–4:44

GETTING STARTED

When is a time that you sensed God was leading you to a new course in your life? What steps did you take to move toward that new calling?

_____

_____

_____

_____

_____

_____

_____

_____

_____

_____

SETTING THE STAGE

For thirty years, Jesus lived in quiet seclusion. Few people knew who He was. But His time of preparation ended when He heard that John the Baptist was preaching the kingdom of heaven was at hand. Jesus' heart surely quickened. He knew that His Father's business was the kingdom of heaven. John the Baptist, in essence, was announcing the end of Jesus' private life and the beginning of His public ministry.

How would the nation of Israel know that Jesus was their Messiah? They were hearing John the Baptist talk about the One who was coming who was mightier that he was—"whose sandal strap I am not worthy to loose" (Luke 3:16). This One to come would baptize with fire instead of water. But how would the people know that Jesus was this promised Messiah . . . the One the prophets had spoken of centuries earlier?

Much is made about the uniqueness of John the Baptist: his eccentricity, clothing, diet, and blunt speech. But what attracted people to him and thrilled every Jewish heart was his message. John told the people the Messiah was *at hand* and the kingdom of God was *in their midst*. His words were like an echo of the ancient prophets. It was the first time the people of Israel had heard such a message in 400 years. You can imagine how excited they became. Could it be true? Was it possible the one foretold by the prophets was now among them?

John's baptism of Jesus marked the beginning of Jesus' public ministry. "When all the people were baptized, it came to pass that Jesus also was baptized; and while He prayed, the heaven was opened" (Luke 3:21). The time had come for Jesus to leave behind the comfort and familiarity of Nazareth and devote Himself to the special work to which God had called Him.

EXPLORING THE TEXT

John the Baptist Prepares the Way (Luke 3:1–11)

¹ Now in the fifteenth year of the reign of Tiberius Caesar, Pontius Pilate being governor of Judea, Herod being tetrarch of Galilee, his brother Philip tetrarch of Iturea and the region of Trachonitis, and Lysanias tetrarch of Abilene, ² while Annas and Caiaphas were high priests, the word of God came to John the son of Zacharias in the wilderness. ³ And he went into all the region around the Jordan,

preaching a baptism of repentance for the remission of sins, [4] as it is written in the book of the words of Isaiah the prophet, saying:

> "The voice of one crying in the wilderness:
> 'Prepare the way of the Lord;
> Make His paths straight.
> [5] Every valley shall be filled
> And every mountain and hill brought low;
> The crooked places shall be made straight
> And the rough ways smooth;
> [6] And all flesh shall see the salvation of God.' "

[7] Then he said to the multitudes that came out to be baptized by him, "Brood of vipers! Who warned you to flee from the wrath to come? [8] Therefore bear fruits worthy of repentance, and do not begin to say to yourselves, 'We have Abraham as our father.' For I say to you that God is able to raise up children to Abraham from these stones. [9] And even now the ax is laid to the root of the trees. Therefore every tree which does not bear good fruit is cut down and thrown into the fire."

[10] So the people asked him, saying, "What shall we do then?"

[11] He answered and said to them, "He who has two tunics, let him give to him who has none; and he who has food, let him do likewise."

---

1. Read Isaiah 40:3–5. How did Luke see John the Baptist as the fulfillment of this prophecy (see Luke 3:4–6)?

_____

_____

_____

_____

_____

2. How would you describe John the Baptist's style in calling people to repentance (see verses 7–9)? Why do you think he took this approach?

_____

_____

_____

_____

_____

_____

_____

_____

_____

The Baptism of Jesus (Luke 3:15–22)

15 Now as the people were in expectation, and all reasoned in their hearts about John, whether he was the Christ or not, 16 John answered, saying to all, "I indeed baptize you with water; but One mightier than I is coming, whose sandal strap I am not worthy to loose. He will baptize you with the Holy Spirit and fire. 17 His winnowing fan is in His hand, and He will thoroughly clean out His threshing floor, and gather the wheat into His barn; but the chaff He will burn with unquenchable fire."

18 And with many other exhortations he preached to the people. 19 But Herod the tetrarch, being rebuked by him concerning Herodias, his brother Philip's wife, and for all the evils which Herod had done, 20 also added this, above all, that he shut John up in prison.

21 When all the people were baptized, it came to pass that Jesus also was baptized; and while He prayed, the heaven was opened. 22 And the Holy Spirit descended in bodily form like a dove upon Him, and a voice came from heaven which said, "You are My beloved Son; in You I am well pleased."

3. How did John compare himself to Jesus? What did he say that Jesus would come to do (see verses 15–17)?

_____

_____

_____

_____

_____

4. How did the Holy Spirit and God the Father prepare Jesus for His earthly ministry (see verses 21–22)? What effect do you imagine this had on Jesus as He assumed His role as the Messiah?

_____

_____

_____

_____

Satan Tempts Jesus (Luke 4:1–15)

¹ Then Jesus, being filled with the Holy Spirit, returned from the Jordan and was led by the Spirit into the wilderness, ² being tempted for forty days by the devil. And in those days He ate nothing, and afterward, when they had ended, He was hungry.

³ And the devil said to Him, "If You are the Son of God, command this stone to become bread."

⁴ But Jesus answered him, saying, "It is written, 'Man shall not live by bread alone, but by every word of God.' "

⁵ Then the devil, taking Him up on a high mountain, showed Him all the kingdoms of the world in a moment of time. ⁶ And the devil said to Him, "All this authority I will give You, and their glory; for this has been delivered to me, and I give it to whomever I wish. ⁷ Therefore, if You will worship before me, all will be Yours."

⁸ And Jesus answered and said to him, "Get behind Me, Satan! For it is written, 'You shall worship the Lord your God, and Him only you shall serve.' "

⁹ Then he brought Him to Jerusalem, set Him on the pinnacle of the temple, and said to Him, "If You are the Son of God, throw Yourself down from here. ¹⁰ For it is written:

'He shall give His angels charge over you,
To keep you,'

¹¹ and,

'In their hands they shall bear you up,
Lest you dash your foot against a stone.' "

¹² And Jesus answered and said to him, "It has been said, 'You shall not tempt the Lord your God.' "

¹³ Now when the devil had ended every temptation, he departed from Him until an opportune time.

¹⁴ Then Jesus returned in the power of the Spirit to Galilee, and news of Him went out through all the surrounding region. ¹⁵ And He taught in their synagogues, being glorified by all.

---

5. Jesus was coming off of a spiritual mountaintop experience. After His baptism, the Father had expressed great pleasure in Him. Then Jesus was led into the wilderness, where Satan tempted Him for forty days. What does this suggest about the way Satan works?

_____

_____

_____

_____

6. How did Jesus resist each of the devil's three temptations (see verses 4, 8, 12)?

_____

_____

_____

_____

_____

_____

_____

Jesus Is Rejected at Nazareth (Luke 4:16–30)

¹⁶ So He came to Nazareth, where He had been brought up. And as His custom was, He went into the synagogue on the Sabbath day, and stood up to read. ¹⁷ And He was handed the book of the prophet Isaiah. And when He had opened the book, He found the place where it was written:

> ¹⁸ "The Spirit of the Lord is upon Me,
> Because He has anointed Me
> To preach the gospel to the poor;
> He has sent Me to heal the brokenhearted,
> To proclaim liberty to the captives
> And recovery of sight to the blind,
> To set at liberty those who are oppressed;
> ¹⁹ To proclaim the acceptable year of the Lord."

²⁰ Then He closed the book, and gave it back to the attendant and sat down. And the eyes of all who were in the synagogue were fixed on Him. ²¹ And He began to say to them, "Today this Scripture is fulfilled in your hearing." ²² So all bore witness to Him, and marveled at the gracious words which proceeded out of His mouth. And they said, "Is this not Joseph's son?"

²³ He said to them, "You will surely say this proverb to Me, 'Physician, heal yourself! Whatever we have heard done in Capernaum, do also here in Your country.' " ²⁴ Then He said, "Assuredly, I say to you, no prophet is accepted in his own country. ²⁵ But I tell you truly, many widows were in Israel in the days of Elijah, when the heaven was shut up three years and six months, and there was a great famine throughout all the land; ²⁶ but to none of them was Elijah sent except to Zarephath, in the region of Sidon, to a woman who was a widow. ²⁷ And many lepers were in Israel in the time of Elisha the prophet, and none of them was cleansed except Naaman the Syrian."

²⁸ So all those in the synagogue, when they heard these things, were filled with wrath, ²⁹ and rose up and thrust Him out of the city; and they led Him to the brow of the hill on which their city was built, that they might throw Him down over the cliff. ³⁰ Then passing through the midst of them, He went His way.

---

7. What did the people of Nazareth say when they looked at Jesus (see verse 22)? What did this tell you about the way they viewed Him?

8. What did Jesus say to the people in His hometown when they rejected Him? Why do you think this incited them to the point they tried to kill Him (see verses 23–29)?

REVIEWING THE STORY

The Bible says little about the first thirty years of Jesus' life. We can assume that Jesus prepared Himself during that time, as He was certainly ready for the ministry that His Father had in store for Him when the time arrived. Jesus embraced His baptism and His Father's words of affirmation. He expertly countered the devil's temptations with words of Scripture that He had memorized. He spoke with authority in the synagogue. He stood firm in the face of rejection at His hometown in Nazareth. When the people rose up and tried to throw Him off a cliff on the outskirts of the village, Jesus escaped their grasp and went His way.

9. When the people asked John the Baptist how they should respond to his message, what did he tell them (see Luke 3:10–11)?

_____

_____

_____

_____

_____

10. How were the three persons of the Trinity—God the Father, God the Son, and God the Holy Spirit—represented at Jesus' baptism (see Luke 3:21–22)?

_____

_____

_____

_____

_____

_____

11. Read Luke 4:13 and 1 Peter 5:8. Why was it important for Jesus to stay vigilant, even after He resisted the devil's three temptations and sent the tempter away in defeat?

_____

_____

_____

_____

_____

_____

12. Jesus used the words of Isaiah 61:1–2 to announce His purpose (see Luke 4:17–21). In your own words, how would you summarize the nature of Jesus' mission?

_____

_____

_____

_____

_____

APPLYING THE MESSAGE

13. In what areas are you most susceptible to temptation? How can you improve your defenses against the devil's schemes? What does James 4:7 promise will happen if you resist the devil?

_____

_____

_____

_____

_____

14. What have you found to be the best strategy for dealing with other people's rejection of your belief in Christ?

REFLECTING ON THE MEANING

At the shores of the Jordan River, John resisted baptizing Jesus because he felt that he had no right to do so. In Jesus, John saw a majesty, purity, and peace that gave him a sense of unworthiness. So, why did Jesus submit to being baptized by John?

One reason is that Jesus wanted to associate Himself with the plight of sinners. Unlike everyone else who came to John to be baptized, He had no sins to confess. He was the perfect Son of God. He was baptized to identify with the race whom He had come to redeem.

Jesus' baptism also served as a public announcement at the outset of His ministry that He had come to be the world's sin-bearer and Savior. Baptism was the public demonstration of Jesus' willingness to assume the burden of sin for the whole world. He was not acknowledging that *He* had sinned. He was acknowledging His willingness to be identified with sinners.

So Jesus went to the place where John baptized sinners. He walked into the dirty waters of the Jordan River in His sinless purity as if to say, "I am the perfect Son of God. But I have come to be a part of this sinful world so that I might redeem those who need to be redeemed." In 2 Corinthians 5:21, Paul writes, "[God] made Him who knew no sin to be sin for us, that we might become the righteousness of God in Him." Jesus faced constant criticism because He associated with the sinners of his day. Yet sinners were the very reason He came to earth.

Jesus' actions challenge anyone who thinks a Christian's entire life should be lived within the context of the church. How can you expect to win people to Christ if you never spend time with them? How can you be an effective witness for Christ if all your friends are Christians?

Journaling Your Response

What are some opportunities you currently have to spend time with those who need to hear about the message of Christ? What will you do to take advantage of those opportunities?

_____

_____

_____

_____

_____

_____

_____

_____

_____

_____

_____

_____

_____

_____

_____

_____

_____

_____

_____

_____

_____

_____

FOUR MEN AND A SAVIOR

Luke 5:1–6:49

GETTING STARTED

How did you respond when you first sensed God's call on your life?

_____

_____

_____

_____

_____

_____

_____

_____

_____

_____

_____

_____

_____

SETTING THE STAGE

A crowd of people gathered to hear the word of God as Jesus stood by the Lake of Gennesaret (also known as the Sea of Galilee). The narrow shoreline made it difficult for many people to get close enough to hear

Jesus. To solve the problem, Jesus commandeered a boat that belonged to a man named Simon (later called Peter).

After Jesus had taught for a while, He gave this command to Peter: "Launch out into the deep and let down your nets for a catch" (Luke 5:4). The Lord knew that Peter and his fellow workers had been fishing all night but caught nothing. He also knew how His instructions would play out in Peter's mind: *Here's a carpenter telling a group of experienced fishermen, who have toiled all night, "All you need to do is launch out into the deep."*

In Israel, fish school in the shallow waters at night. When the sun comes out, they head for the deep waters, where they are not easy to catch. That is why the people of Jesus' day fished at night on the Sea of Galilee. But notice that Jesus said to Peter, "Let down your *nets* (plural) for a catch." Jesus was anticipating a great catch of fish.

Peter replied, "Master, we've toiled all night and caught nothing; nevertheless at Your word I will let down *the* net" (verse 5, emphasis added). In other words, Peter was saying, "I'm going to obey in the cheapest, easiest way I can. I'm not going to unfurl all these nets and string them out because nothing's going to happen. But I will lower one to make you happy." Peter's obedience wasn't complete. And he wasn't prepared for what was about to happen.

Simon Peter and his crew caught so many fish that their net (singular) started to break and their boat began to sink. Simon then fell down at Jesus' knees and cried, "Depart from me, for I am a sinful man, O Lord!" (verse 8).

Exploring the Text

Four Fisherman Called As Disciples (Luke 5:1–11)

¹ So it was, as the multitude pressed about Him to hear the word of God, that He stood by the Lake of Gennesaret, ² and saw two boats standing by the lake; but the fishermen had gone from them and were washing their nets. ³ Then He got into one of the boats, which

was Simon's, and asked him to put out a little from the land. And He sat down and taught the multitudes from the boat.

⁴ When He had stopped speaking, He said to Simon, "Launch out into the deep and let down your nets for a catch."

⁵ But Simon answered and said to Him, "Master, we have toiled all night and caught nothing; nevertheless at Your word I will let down the net." ⁶ And when they had done this, they caught a great number of fish, and their net was breaking. ⁷ So they signaled to their partners in the other boat to come and help them. And they came and filled both the boats, so that they began to sink. ⁸ When Simon Peter saw it, he fell down at Jesus' knees, saying, "Depart from me, for I am a sinful man, O Lord!"

⁹ For he and all who were with him were astonished at the catch of fish which they had taken; ¹⁰ and so also were James and John, the sons of Zebedee, who were partners with Simon. And Jesus said to Simon, "Do not be afraid. From now on you will catch men." ¹¹ So when they had brought their boats to land, they forsook all and followed Him.

---

1. What request did Jesus make of Simon (Peter)? How did Peter respond (see verses 4–5)?

_____

_____

_____

_____

2. How did the four fishermen react to Jesus' invitation to "catch men" (verse 10)? What does this tell you about this group of men whom Jesus had called to follow Him?

_____

_____

_____

Jesus Forgives and Heals a Paralytic (Luke 5:17–26)

[17] Now it happened on a certain day, as He was teaching, that there were Pharisees and teachers of the law sitting by, who had come out of every town of Galilee, Judea, and Jerusalem. And the power of the Lord was present to heal them. [18] Then behold, men brought on a bed a man who was paralyzed, whom they sought to bring in and lay before Him. [19] And when they could not find how they might bring him in, because of the crowd, they went up on the housetop and let him down with his bed through the tiling into the midst before Jesus.

[20] When He saw their faith, He said to him, "Man, your sins are forgiven you."

[21] And the scribes and the Pharisees began to reason, saying, "Who is this who speaks blasphemies? Who can forgive sins but God alone?"

[22] But when Jesus perceived their thoughts, He answered and said to them, "Why are you reasoning in your hearts? [23] Which is easier, to say, 'Your sins are forgiven you,' or to say, 'Rise up and walk'? [24] But that you may know that the Son of Man has power on earth to forgive sins"—He said to the man who was paralyzed, "I say to you, arise, take up your bed, and go to your house."

[25] Immediately he rose up before them, took up what he had been lying on, and departed to his own house, glorifying God. [26] And they were all amazed, and they glorified God and were filled with fear, saying, "We have seen strange things today!"

3. How were the men able to get their paralyzed friend into the presence of Jesus? What prompted Jesus to forgive and heal the paralyzed man (see verses 18–20)?

4. What objections did Jesus' critics raise about His ministry? How did Jesus respond to their complaints (see verses 21–24)?

_____

_____

_____

The Sermon on the Plain (Luke 6:12–26)

¹²Now it came to pass in those days that He went out to the mountain to pray, and continued all night in prayer to God. ¹³And when it was day, He called His disciples to Himself; and from them He chose twelve whom He also named apostles: ¹⁴Simon, whom He also named Peter, and Andrew his brother; James and John; Philip and Bartholomew; ¹⁵Matthew and Thomas; James the son of Alphaeus, and Simon called the Zealot; ¹⁶Judas the son of James, and Judas Iscariot who also became a traitor.

¹⁷And He came down with them and stood on a level place with a crowd of His disciples and a great multitude of people from all Judea and Jerusalem, and from the seacoast of Tyre and Sidon, who came to hear Him and be healed of their diseases, ¹⁸as well as those who were tormented with unclean spirits. And they were healed. ¹⁹And the whole multitude sought to touch Him, for power went out from Him and healed them all.

²⁰Then He lifted up His eyes toward His disciples, and said:

"Blessed are you poor,
For yours is the kingdom of God.
²¹Blessed are you who hunger now,
For you shall be filled.
Blessed are you who weep now,
For you shall laugh.
²²Blessed are you when men hate you,

And when they exclude you,

And revile you, and cast out your name as evil,

For the Son of Man's sake.

23 Rejoice in that day and leap for joy!

For indeed your reward is great in heaven,

For in like manner their fathers did to the prophets.

24 "But woe to you who are rich,

For you have received your consolation.

25 Woe to you who are full,

For you shall hunger.

Woe to you who laugh now,

For you shall mourn and weep.

26 Woe to you when all men speak well of you,

For so did their fathers to the false prophets."

---

5. What do you learn in this passage about Jesus' prayer habits (see verse 12)?

_____

_____

_____

_____

_____

6. What type of people did Jesus say in this passage were blessed (see verses 20–22)?

_____

_____

_____

_____

_____

Love Your Enemies (Luke 6:27–38)

[27] "But I say to you who hear: Love your enemies, do good to those who hate you, [28] bless those who curse you, and pray for those who spitefully use you. [29] To him who strikes you on the one cheek, offer the other also. And from him who takes away your cloak, do not withhold your tunic either. [30] Give to everyone who asks of you. And from him who takes away your goods do not ask them back. [31] And just as you want men to do to you, you also do to them likewise.

[32] "But if you love those who love you, what credit is that to you? For even sinners love those who love them. [33] And if you do good to those who do good to you, what credit is that to you? For even sinners do the same. [34] And if you lend to those from whom you hope to receive back, what credit is that to you? For even sinners lend to sinners to receive as much back. [35] But love your enemies, do good, and lend, hoping for nothing in return; and your reward will be great, and you will be sons of the Most High. For He is kind to the unthankful and evil. [36] Therefore be merciful, just as your Father also is merciful.

[37] "Judge not, and you shall not be judged. Condemn not, and you shall not be condemned. Forgive, and you will be forgiven. [38] Give, and it will be given to you: good measure, pressed down, shaken together, and running over will be put into your bosom. For with the same measure that you use, it will be measured back to you."

---

7. The Law of Moses taught that the people should love their neighbors as they loved themselves (see Leviticus 19:18). How did Jesus take this a step further (see verses 27–31)?

_____

_____

_____

_____

8. What commands did Jesus give about judging others? What kind of mercy did Jesus expect His disciples to demonstrate to others (see verses 37–38)?

_____

_____

_____

_____

Reviewing the Story

In Luke 5–6, we see glimpses of Jesus' values, power, and authority. He showed the four fishermen (who later became His disciples) why it was a good idea to obey His commands to the letter. He showed a leper and a paralyzed man what His healing power could accomplish, and in the process revealed to the Pharisees why it was a bad idea to challenge Him. He showed a paralyzed man that He could meet spiritual needs as well by forgiving the man's sins. He taught His followers to go beyond the Law of Moses and love their enemies, do good to those who hated them, bless those who cursed them, and pray for those who spitefully used them.

9. How would you describe the response as word began to spread about Jesus' teachings and His ability to heal people of diseases and disabilities (see Luke 5:1)?

_____

_____

_____

_____

10. What evidence can you find in the healing of the paralyzed man that Jesus claimed to be God (see Luke 5:20–24)?

_____

_____

_____

11. What kinds of people did Jesus warn in Luke 6:24–26?

_____

_____

_____

12. According to Jesus, what responses should His followers have toward those who hate them (see Luke 6:27–36)?

_____

_____

_____

APPLYING THE MESSAGE

13. Peter found it difficult (after fishing all night and catching nothing) to follow Jesus' instruction to launch out again and put down the nets. When have you faced an instruction from God that you found difficult to follow? What happened when you chose to obey?

_____

_____

_____

14. How does it feel to know that you are going to be judged by the same measure with which you judge others?

_____

_____

_____

REFLECTING ON THE MEANING

Because God's call is supernatural, many people assume it involves super-natural occurrences. They look for some mysterious thing to happen . . . some aura to enshroud them. But God's call often comes in the ordinary things of life. Jesus used a boat to teach Peter a lesson. He used fishing to illustrate His call on Peter's life. He called one woman by a well. He called others in the temple. If you're looking for some bright star in the sky or some overwhelming emotional experience, you may not hear the call of God. He calls you in the everyday events of your life.

God's call demands your obedient response. You can miss some of God's blessing if you don't listen to what He says and then obey. The Lord said to Peter, "Let down your nets." Peter said, "Lord, I'm going to let down *one* net." As a result, Peter almost sank two boats because he didn't do what the Lord said. If he had let down *all* the nets, he would have caught a lot more fish. When the Lord says, "Let down the nets," don't let down just one.

Likewise, when God calls you to serve Him, don't worry about what you might have to sacrifice. When Peter preached on the Day of Pentecost and saw 3,000 people get saved, it's doubtful that he turned to Andrew and said, "I really miss the nets and boats and smelly old fish." God's call is an upward call. It's always to something greater and more exciting than anything you can ever imagine.

God knows what is best for you, and He longs to see you on the path of obedience. He doesn't call you to follow Him to make your life difficult but to grant to you the most wonderful joy that is available to a person on this earth.

JOURNALING YOUR RESPONSE

In what area of your life are you "one-netting" it—that is, holding back (as Peter did) from a full and sacrificial commitment to the Lord's will?

PEOPLE ARE IMPORTANT

Luke 7:1–8:56

GETTING STARTED

What are some of the most significant changes you can see in your life over the past ten years?

_____

_____

_____

_____

_____

_____

_____

_____

_____

_____

_____

_____

_____

_____

_____

_____

_____

_____

SETTING THE STAGE

The Gospel of Luke contains thirty-five parables of Jesus. Nineteen of those parables are unique to Luke's Gospel. They reveal great truths of love, grace, forgiveness, and the human element that captures our attention. They also reveal a doctor's touch. Luke was a physician, and it is clear from his words that he looked with compassion at people. As he told the stories of Jesus' interaction with those who needed His touch, he told them through the eyes of a loving and caring person and included many details that make the stories come alive.

The stories Jesus told were not for entertainment nor to fill the pages of the Gospels. Jesus never told a story without a specific purpose behind it. His word pictures were mighty weapons that He used to fill the minds of His hearers with truth they would never forget. He did not tell stories for spectacular reasons. When He told stories, He took a truth that might not be otherwise understood and presented it in a way that could be comprehended by His listeners. His word pictures made that truth come alive in the lives of His people. These word pictures also frustrated His enemies, who were often unable to decipher them.

The setting of the story of the two debtors, which is the first parable that Luke records in his Gospel, is the house of Simon the Pharisee. Be careful not to confuse it with similar stories found in the Gospels of Matthew, Mark, and John, which also mention the very common name Simon. The incident that Luke records in this section of his Gospel took place in a town called Nain. The stories in the other Gospels took place in Bethany.

EXPLORING THE TEXT

Jesus Heals a Servant and Raises a Widow's Son (Luke 7:1–17)

[1] Now when He concluded all His sayings in the hearing of the people, He entered Capernaum. [2] And a certain centurion's servant, who was

dear to him, was sick and ready to die. [3] So when he heard about Jesus, he sent elders of the Jews to Him, pleading with Him to come and heal his servant. [4] And when they came to Jesus, they begged Him earnestly, saying that the one for whom He should do this was deserving, [5] "for he loves our nation, and has built us a synagogue."

[6] Then Jesus went with them. And when He was already not far from the house, the centurion sent friends to Him, saying to Him, "Lord, do not trouble Yourself, for I am not worthy that You should enter under my roof. [7] Therefore I did not even think myself worthy to come to You. But say the word, and my servant will be healed. [8] For I also am a man placed under authority, having soldiers under me. And I say to one, 'Go,' and he goes; and to another, 'Come,' and he comes; and to my servant, 'Do this,' and he does it."

[9] When Jesus heard these things, He marveled at him, and turned around and said to the crowd that followed Him, "I say to you, I have not found such great faith, not even in Israel!" [10] And those who were sent, returning to the house, found the servant well who had been sick.

[11] Now it happened, the day after, that He went into a city called Nain; and many of His disciples went with Him, and a large crowd. [12] And when He came near the gate of the city, behold, a dead man was being carried out, the only son of his mother; and she was a widow. And a large crowd from the city was with her. [13] When the Lord saw her, He had compassion on her and said to her, "Do not weep." [14] Then He came and touched the open coffin, and those who carried him stood still. And He said, "Young man, I say to you, arise." [15] So he who was dead sat up and began to speak. And He presented him to his mother.

[16] Then fear came upon all, and they glorified God, saying, "A great prophet has risen up among us"; and, "God has visited His people." [17] And this report about Him went throughout all Judea and all the surrounding region.

1. According to the Jewish elders, why did the centurion deserve to have his servant healed (see verses 4–5)?

_____

_____

_____

_____

_____

2. Read 1 Kings 17:17–24 and 2 Kings 4:18–37. Why do you think the people of Nain assumed that Jesus was a prophet (see Luke 7:16)?

_____

_____

_____

_____

_____

Jesus Anointed by a Sinful Woman (Luke 7:36–50)

36 Then one of the Pharisees asked Him to eat with him. And He went to the Pharisee's house, and sat down to eat. 37 And behold, a woman in the city who was a sinner, when she knew that Jesus sat at the table in the Pharisee's house, brought an alabaster flask of fragrant oil, 38 and stood at His feet behind Him weeping; and she began to wash His feet with her tears, and wiped them with the hair of her head; and she kissed His feet and anointed them with the fragrant oil. 39 Now when the Pharisee who had invited Him saw this, he spoke to himself, saying, "This Man, if He were a prophet, would know who and what manner of woman this is who is touching Him, for she is a sinner."

40 And Jesus answered and said to him, "Simon, I have something to say to you."

So he said, "Teacher, say it."

⁴¹ "There was a certain creditor who had two debtors. One owed five hundred denarii, and the other fifty. ⁴² And when they had nothing with which to repay, he freely forgave them both. Tell Me, therefore, which of them will love him more?"

⁴³ Simon answered and said, "I suppose the one whom he forgave more."

And He said to him, "You have rightly judged." ⁴⁴ Then He turned to the woman and said to Simon, "Do you see this woman? I entered your house; you gave Me no water for My feet, but she has washed My feet with her tears and wiped them with the hair of her head. ⁴⁵ You gave Me no kiss, but this woman has not ceased to kiss My feet since the time I came in. ⁴⁶ You did not anoint My head with oil, but this woman has anointed My feet with fragrant oil. ⁴⁷ Therefore I say to you, her sins, which are many, are forgiven, for she loved much. But to whom little is forgiven, the same loves little."

⁴⁸ Then He said to her, "Your sins are forgiven."

⁴⁹ And those who sat at the table with Him began to say to themselves, "Who is this who even forgives sins?"

⁵⁰ Then He said to the woman, "Your faith has saved you. Go in peace."

---

3. The woman in this story took advantage of the social customs of the day that permitted a needy person to visit such a banquet to receive some of the leftovers. But what was the woman's true intent for coming to the Pharisee's house that day (see verses 37–38)?

_____

_____

_____

_____

_____

4. Why did Simon, the Pharisee host, doubt that Jesus was a prophet? How did the parable that Jesus told serve to address Simon's doubts (see verses 39–43)?

_____

_____

_____

_____

_____

_____

Parable of the Sower and Lamp on a Stand (Luke 8:1–18)

¹ Now it came to pass, afterward, that He went through every city and village, preaching and bringing the glad tidings of the kingdom of God. And the twelve were with Him, ² and certain women who had been healed of evil spirits and infirmities—Mary called Magdalene, out of whom had come seven demons, ³ and Joanna the wife of Chuza, Herod's steward, and Susanna, and many others who provided for Him from their substance.

⁴ And when a great multitude had gathered, and they had come to Him from every city, He spoke by a parable: ⁵ "A sower went out to sow his seed. And as he sowed, some fell by the wayside; and it was trampled down, and the birds of the air devoured it. ⁶ Some fell on rock; and as soon as it sprang up, it withered away because it lacked moisture. ⁷ And some fell among thorns, and the thorns sprang up with it and choked it. ⁸ But others fell on good ground, sprang up, and yielded a crop a hundredfold." When He had said these things He cried, "He who has ears to hear, let him hear!"

⁹ Then His disciples asked Him, saying, "What does this parable mean?"

¹⁰ And He said, "To you it has been given to know the mysteries of the kingdom of God, but to the rest it is given in parables, that

'Seeing they may not see,

And hearing they may not understand.'

11 "Now the parable is this: The seed is the word of God. 12 Those by the wayside are the ones who hear; then the devil comes and takes away the word out of their hearts, lest they should believe and be saved. 13 But the ones on the rock are those who, when they hear, receive the word with joy; and these have no root, who believe for a while and in time of temptation fall away. 14 Now the ones that fell among thorns are those who, when they have heard, go out and are choked with cares, riches, and pleasures of life, and bring no fruit to maturity. 15 But the ones that fell on the good ground are those who, having heard the word with a noble and good heart, keep it and bear fruit with patience.

16 "No one, when he has lit a lamp, covers it with a vessel or puts it under a bed, but sets it on a lampstand, that those who enter may see the light. 17 For nothing is secret that will not be revealed, nor anything hidden that will not be known and come to light. 18 Therefore take heed how you hear. For whoever has, to him more will be given; and whoever does not have, even what he seems to have will be taken from him."

---

5. Mary Magdalene followed Jesus faithfully and supported His ministry to the very end (see verse 2). Even after most of the disciples had fled, she stayed with Jesus for the duration of His crucifixion. Read John 20:1–16. How did God reward her faithful service?

_____

_____

_____

_____

_____

6. In Jesus' parable of the sower, what do the different soils represent (see Luke 8:11–15)? In the parable of the lamp, what does the light represent (see verses 16–18)?

_____

_____

_____

_____

A Demon-Possessed Man Healed (Luke 8:26–39)

²⁶ Then they sailed to the country of the Gadarenes, which is opposite Galilee. ²⁷ And when He stepped out on the land, there met Him a certain man from the city who had demons for a long time. And he wore no clothes, nor did he live in a house but in the tombs. ²⁸ When he saw Jesus, he cried out, fell down before Him, and with a loud voice said, "What have I to do with You, Jesus, Son of the Most High God? I beg You, do not torment me!" ²⁹ For He had commanded the unclean spirit to come out of the man. For it had often seized him, and he was kept under guard, bound with chains and shackles; and he broke the bonds and was driven by the demon into the wilderness.

³⁰ Jesus asked him, saying, "What is your name?"

And he said, "Legion," because many demons had entered him. ³¹ And they begged Him that He would not command them to go out into the abyss.

³² Now a herd of many swine was feeding there on the mountain. So they begged Him that He would permit them to enter them. And He permitted them. ³³ Then the demons went out of the man and entered the swine, and the herd ran violently down the steep place into the lake and drowned.

³⁴ When those who fed them saw what had happened, they fled and told it in the city and in the country. ³⁵ Then they went out to see what had happened, and came to Jesus, and found the man from whom the demons had departed, sitting at the feet of Jesus, clothed

and in his right mind. And they were afraid. [36] They also who had seen it told them by what means he who had been demon-possessed was healed. [37] Then the whole multitude of the surrounding region of the Gadarenes asked Him to depart from them, for they were seized with great fear. And He got into the boat and returned.

[38] Now the man from whom the demons had departed begged Him that he might be with Him. But Jesus sent him away, saying, [39] "Return to your own house, and tell what great things God has done for you." And he went his way and proclaimed throughout the whole city what great things Jesus had done for him.

---

7. What kind of life did the demon-possessed man endure before he encountered Jesus (see verses 26–30)?

_____

_____

_____

_____

8. How did the people of the village react when they saw the demon-possessed man clothed and in his right mind (see verses 35–37)?

_____

_____

_____

_____

REVIEWING THE STORY

The events recorded in Luke 7–8 reveal that nothing was beyond Jesus' power and authority. The centurion in Capernaum recognized this when he asked Jesus to heal his servant. He knew Christ only had to give the command and his servant would be made well. Jesus rewarded the centurion's faith by healing the servant—just as he had asked. Jesus demonstrated

His authority to forgive sins when He pardoned the transgressions of the woman who washed His feet with her tears. He had authority over the demons who possessed the man in the country of the Gadarenes and cast them into a herd of pigs. Jesus even had authority over death, which held a widow's son in its grip, and commanded the young man to come back to life.

9. The widow of Nain was in a desperate situation. She had lost her only son, who was likely her only means of financial support. She had very little hope for the future. What do Jesus' actions tell you about Him and His ministry (see Luke 7:11–15)?

_____

_____

_____

_____

10. What did Jesus' parable of the two debtors reveal to Simon the Pharisee, who had judged Jesus in his heart for allowing a sinful woman to anoint His feet (see Luke 7:41–43)?

_____

_____

_____

_____

11. How does "good ground" respond to the Word of God (see Luke 8:15)? Is this a description of how you normally respond to God's Word? Explain.

_____

_____

_____

_____

12. Who was Jesus' first missionary to the country of the Gadarenes (see Luke 8:38–39)? Why do you think this man was the ideal person to talk about Jesus?

APPLYING THE MESSAGE

13. The centurion believed that Jesus could heal his servant from a distance with just a word. What do you believe Jesus can do in *your* life?

14. What are some ways that you can actively sow the Word of God today? What are some ways that you can illuminate the message of Jesus to your world?

REFLECTING ON THE MEANING

The narrative of Mary Magdalene in the Gospels begins with her being possessed by seven demons and ends with her having a conversation with the risen Lord before anyone else did. The first, and most obvious, take-away from her story is what Christ can do in a person's life. To get an idea of what Mary Magdalene's life may have been like before she encountered Jesus, look at the story of the demon-possessed man in Luke 8. It's hard to imagine a more miserable existence or a more bleak future. Yet that's the kind of person Jesus met when He met Mary.

A few years later, Jesus emerged from His tomb bearing the greatest news in the history of humankind. The first person to receive the news wasn't Peter, John, or even Jesus' mother, Mary. It was Mary Magdalene, who had the best reason to love Him because of all that she had been forgiven. Of all the men and women then living in the world, the Lord Jesus chose her.

Mary Magdalene also shows us what we can do *for* Christ. Mary probably came from a wealthy family. She pooled her resources with Susanna and another woman to help Jesus with His ministry. The disciples had no means of support. They received no church offerings. They operated on the basis of faith. These women funded the work of Jesus during His ministry.

Finally, Mary became a voice of testimony to the risen Christ. The account she gave of her changed life likely changed the lives of many others. Her story shows that nothing you have done can ever put you beyond the reach of God. The sweetest promises in the Bible are for those who deserve them the least. If the Lord Jesus can change the life of Mary Magdalene, He can change yours.

JOURNALING YOUR RESPONSE

What is the most dramatic change that Jesus has brought about in your life?

WHO IS MY NEIGHBOR?

Luke 9:1–10:42

GETTING STARTED

What comes to mind when you think of "your neighbor"? Do you picture a person on your street, or is your definition broader in nature? Explain.

_____

_____

_____

_____

_____

_____

_____

_____

_____

_____

_____

_____

SETTING THE STAGE

When studying the parables and words of our Lord, it's helpful to recognize how many times His detractors tried to trap Him with their questions. They were always trying to paint Him into a corner. The man who approached

47

Jesus in Luke 10 is called a "lawyer," but literally, he was someone who had studied the Mosaic Law. In our culture today, we would say that he was a theologian. He studied the Scriptures to understand their meaning.

But as we will see, the question this lawyer asked was not sincere. The Bible tells us that his motivation was to tempt, test, or trap Christ. The religious lawyers of Jesus' day loved to discuss the urgent social problems that were all around them. However, they never wanted to do anything *about* those problems. They would discuss them in the abstract and slant their discussions to evade any action on their part or any feeling of responsibility.

The lawyer who spoke to Jesus had sufficient knowledge of the Scriptures. In fact, when Jesus asked him a question, the man was able to recite the most important commandments of the Old Testament from memory. But he did not know how to apply those truths. He had never loved his neighbor. Otherwise, he would have known the *identity* of his neighbor. You can't love your neighbor and not know who that person is!

So when the lawyer asked Jesus, "Who is my neighbor?" he gave himself away. He demonstrated that he had information, but that information never took hold in his heart.

EXPLORING THE TEXT

The Feeding of the 5,000 and Peter's Confession (Luke 9:10–22)

---

¹⁰ And the apostles, when they had returned, told Him all that they had done. Then He took them and went aside privately into a deserted place belonging to the city called Bethsaida. ¹¹ But when the multitudes knew it, they followed Him; and He received them and spoke to them about the kingdom of God, and healed those who had need of healing. ¹² When the day began to wear away, the twelve came and said to Him, "Send the multitude away, that they may go into the surrounding towns and country, and lodge and get provisions; for we are in a deserted place here."

¹³ But He said to them, "You give them something to eat."

And they said, "We have no more than five loaves and two fish, unless we go and buy food for all these people." [14] For there were about five thousand men.

Then He said to His disciples, "Make them sit down in groups of fifty." [15] And they did so, and made them all sit down.

[16] Then He took the five loaves and the two fish, and looking up to heaven, He blessed and broke them, and gave them to the disciples to set before the multitude. [17] So they all ate and were filled, and twelve baskets of the leftover fragments were taken up by them.

[18] And it happened, as He was alone praying, that His disciples joined Him, and He asked them, saying, "Who do the crowds say that I am?"

[19] So they answered and said, "John the Baptist, but some say Elijah; and others say that one of the old prophets has risen again."

[20] He said to them, "But who do you say that I am?"

Peter answered and said, "The Christ of God."

[21] And He strictly warned and commanded them to tell this to no one, [22] saying, "The Son of Man must suffer many things, and be rejected by the elders and chief priests and scribes, and be killed, and be raised the third day."

---

1. Jesus withdrew with the disciples to the town of Bethsaida for a time of rest, but the crowds followed when they learned He was there. How did Jesus react to the intrusion? What was the disciples' attitude toward the people (see verses 11–12)?

_____

_____

_____

_____

_____

_____

2. According to the disciples, who did the crowds believe that Jesus was (see verse 19)? Why do you think so many people followed Jesus without realizing His true identity?

_____

_____

_____

_____

_____

The Cost of Following Jesus (Luke 9:46–62)

46 Then a dispute arose among them as to which of them would be greatest. 47 And Jesus, perceiving the thought of their heart, took a little child and set him by Him, 48 and said to them, "Whoever receives this little child in My name receives Me; and whoever receives Me receives Him who sent Me. For he who is least among you all will be great."

49 Now John answered and said, "Master, we saw someone casting out demons in Your name, and we forbade him because he does not follow with us."

50 But Jesus said to him, "Do not forbid him, for he who is not against us is on our side."

51 Now it came to pass, when the time had come for Him to be received up, that He steadfastly set His face to go to Jerusalem, 52 and sent messengers before His face. And as they went, they entered a village of the Samaritans, to prepare for Him. 53 But they did not receive Him, because His face was set for the journey to Jerusalem. 54 And when His disciples James and John saw this, they said, "Lord, do You want us to command fire to come down from heaven and consume them, just as Elijah did?"

55 But He turned and rebuked them, and said, "You do not know what manner of spirit you are of. 56 For the Son of Man did not come

to destroy men's lives but to save them." And they went to another village.

⁵⁷ Now it happened as they journeyed on the road, that someone said to Him, "Lord, I will follow You wherever You go."

⁵⁸ And Jesus said to him, "Foxes have holes and birds of the air have nests, but the Son of Man has nowhere to lay His head."

⁵⁹ Then He said to another, "Follow Me."

But he said, "Lord, let me first go and bury my father."

⁶⁰ Jesus said to him, "Let the dead bury their own dead, but you go and preach the kingdom of God."

⁶¹ And another also said, "Lord, I will follow You, but let me first go and bid them farewell who are at my house."

⁶² But Jesus said to him, "No one, having put his hand to the plow, and looking back, is fit for the kingdom of God."

---

3. Roman law in the first century gave the father absolute power over his family, which meant that children had no legal status. How did Jesus use the example of a child to show the disciples what it meant to be great in God's kingdom (see verses 46–48)?

_____

_____

_____

_____

4. How would you describe the kind of commitment that Jesus expected of those who chose to follow Him (see verses 57–62)?

_____

_____

_____

_____

Jesus Sends Out the Seventy (Luke 10:1–20)

¹ After these things the Lord appointed seventy others also, and sent them two by two before His face into every city and place where He Himself was about to go. ² Then He said to them, "The harvest truly is great, but the laborers are few; therefore pray the Lord of the harvest to send out laborers into His harvest. ³ Go your way; behold, I send you out as lambs among wolves. ⁴ Carry neither money bag, knapsack, nor sandals; and greet no one along the road. ⁵ But whatever house you enter, first say, 'Peace to this house.' ⁶ And if a son of peace is there, your peace will rest on it; if not, it will return to you. ⁷ And remain in the same house, eating and drinking such things as they give, for the laborer is worthy of his wages. Do not go from house to house. ⁸ Whatever city you enter, and they receive you, eat such things as are set before you. ⁹ And heal the sick there, and say to them, 'The kingdom of God has come near to you.' ¹⁰ But whatever city you enter, and they do not receive you, go out into its streets and say, ¹¹ 'The very dust of your city which clings to us we wipe off against you. Nevertheless know this, that the kingdom of God has come near you.' ¹² But I say to you that it will be more tolerable in that Day for Sodom than for that city.

¹³ "Woe to you, Chorazin! Woe to you, Bethsaida! For if the mighty works which were done in you had been done in Tyre and Sidon, they would have repented long ago, sitting in sackcloth and ashes. ¹⁴ But it will be more tolerable for Tyre and Sidon at the judgment than for you. ¹⁵ And you, Capernaum, who are exalted to heaven, will be brought down to Hades. ¹⁶ He who hears you hears Me, he who rejects you rejects Me, and he who rejects Me rejects Him who sent Me."

¹⁷ Then the seventy returned with joy, saying, "Lord, even the demons are subject to us in Your name."

¹⁸ And He said to them, "I saw Satan fall like lightning from heaven. ¹⁹ Behold, I give you the authority to trample on serpents

and scorpions, and over all the power of the enemy, and nothing shall by any means hurt you. [20] Nevertheless do not rejoice in this, that the spirits are subject to you, but rather rejoice because your names are written in heaven."

---

5. Why do you think Jesus sent out His followers in pairs? What were they to do? What responsibility did Jesus give to them (see verses 1–11)?

_____

_____

_____

_____

6. Look at Ezekiel 26–28. What fate was Jesus warning Chorazin and Bethsaida about when He compared them to Tyre and Sidon?

_____

_____

_____

_____

The Parable of the Good Samaritan (Luke 10:25–37)

[25] And behold, a certain lawyer stood up and tested Him, saying, "Teacher, what shall I do to inherit eternal life?"

[26] He said to him, "What is written in the law? What is your reading of it?"

[27] So he answered and said, " 'You shall love the Lord your God with all your heart, with all your soul, with all your strength, and with all your mind,' and 'your neighbor as yourself.' "

[28] And He said to him, "You have answered rightly; do this and you will live."

[29] But he, wanting to justify himself, said to Jesus, "And who is my neighbor?"

³⁰ Then Jesus answered and said: "A certain man went down from Jerusalem to Jericho, and fell among thieves, who stripped him of his clothing, wounded him, and departed, leaving him half dead. ³¹ Now by chance a certain priest came down that road. And when he saw him, he passed by on the other side.³² Likewise a Levite, when he arrived at the place, came and looked, and passed by on the other side. ³³ But a certain Samaritan, as he journeyed, came where he was. And when he saw him, he had compassion. ³⁴ So he went to him and bandaged his wounds, pouring on oil and wine; and he set him on his own animal, brought him to an inn, and took care of him. ³⁵ On the next day, when he departed, he took out two denarii, gave them to the innkeeper, and said to him, 'Take care of him; and whatever more you spend, when I come again, I will repay you.' ³⁶ So which of these three do you think was neighbor to him who fell among the thieves?"

³⁷ And he said, "He who showed mercy on him."

Then Jesus said to him, "Go and do likewise."

---

7. Contrast how the Samaritan treated the wounded man with how the priest and Levite did. What did it cost the Samaritan to show compassion on the man (see verses 30–36)?

----

8. In Jesus' parable, the injured man was Jewish, as were the first two people to pass him by. All three of them would have refused to associate with the Samaritan (see verses 31–32). With that in mind, how would you answer the man's question, "And who is my neighbor?"

REVIEWING THE STORY

Jesus often challenged His listeners (and His own disciples) about the types of people they should consider their "neighbors." When the disciples wanted Jesus to send away the crowd of people near Bethsaida who had gathered to hear Him speak, Christ told them give them something to eat . . . and then miraculously provided for everyone. Jesus spoke openly of the cost involved in following Him and sent His followers out two-by-two to gain practical experience on how to serve their "neighbors." And when a lawyer asked Jesus outright whom he should consider his neighbor, Jesus responded with a parable that reveals our responsibility as His followers is to extend mercy to those in need—no matter who they are.

9. The disciples wanted to send the hungry multitude away and let the people take care of their own needs. What does Jesus' response tell you about what He expects from all of His followers (see Luke 9:13)?

_____

_____

_____

_____

_____

_____

10. What evidence do you see that suggests the disciples weren't quite ready to continue Jesus' ministry on their own (see Luke 9:46–54)?

_____

_____

_____

_____

_____

_____

11. What happened when the seventy workers Jesus sent out obeyed His instructions regarding their ministry (see Luke 10:17–20)?

_____

_____

_____

_____

_____

_____

12. What did the Samaritan do that Jesus wanted His followers to do likewise (see Luke 10:37)?

_____

_____

_____

_____

_____

APPLYING THE MESSAGE

13. The people in Jesus' day had all kinds of excuses for why they couldn't drop everything and follow Christ. What are some excuses that people give today for refusing to follow Jesus?

_____

_____

_____

_____

_____

_____

14. What is the best way to approach an unbeliever with the good news of Jesus? What is the best way to respond when people reject the message of the gospel?

_____

_____

_____

_____

REFLECTING ON THE MEANING

As we look at the actions of the good Samaritan, there are several points that stand out. The first is that his love showed great compassion. The priest, the Levite, and the Samaritan all looked at the injured traveler. But only the Samaritan saw him through eyes of compassion.

In the New Testament, *compassion* means "a deep moving within the inward spirit." Matthew uses the word three times in his Gospel to describe Jesus' reaction to the masses of people. In each situation, Jesus' compassion was triggered by a physical need He observed in the people's lives. In Matthew 9:36, Jesus saw the masses as weary and scattered. In Matthew 14:14, He saw them as sick, needing to be healed. In Matthew 15:32, He saw them as hungry, needing to eat. When Jesus saw broken humanity, His heart was moved with compassion.

The Samaritan looked at the broken traveler through the eyes of Jesus and had compassion on him. His love involved *great risk*. The thieves who had attacked the traveler might still have been around. Yet he risked his own safety and well-being to help someone else.

His love also showed *great mercy*. He cleansed the injured traveler's wounds with wine. He soothed the wounds by pouring oil on them. He bound the wounds so they could begin to heal. He delivered his love with care.

The Samaritan's love also involved *great cost*. He gave his animal to the traveler while he walked. He gave his time by postponing his own schedule two days so he could stay with the traveler. He gave his money to pay for the traveler's recovery at the inn.

Love will cost you something. Jesus said if you want to be a neighbor, love like the Samaritan loved. Love sacrificially.

JOURNALING YOUR RESPONSE

Aside from Jesus, who has modeled sacrificial love for you?

A MASTER CLASS IN PRAYER

Luke 11:1–12:59

GETTING STARTED

What are some situations that you are currently taking to God in prayer? How have you seen God move in your life as a result of your prayers?

_____

_____

_____

_____

_____

_____

_____

_____

_____

SETTING THE STAGE

Discouragement is a recurring theme in the lives of the disciples. They encountered all manner of fraudulent followers of Christ and were constantly tempted to do something about those who claimed to be disciples but did not live the life. Many believers today experience similar emotions. It can be extremely discouraging for Christians to look around at those who bear the name of Christ but seem to show no evidence in their daily lives that they are Christians.

This realization can be doubly discouraging when it involves Christian leaders, respected teachers or authors, and other well-known believers. In the eyes of many unbelievers, these people represent Christianity. When they are shown to be hypocrites, the cause of outreach is set back tremendously. Many faithful believers feel as though they have to work harder just to overcome the prejudices created by the hypocrisy of others.

Jesus understood this, and He spoke forcefully against people who followed their own agenda while pretending to follow Scripture. He warned His disciples, "Beware of the leaven of the Pharisees, which is hypocrisy" (Luke 12:1). Jesus emphasized that His disciples should not be discouraged, because people's true motives will one day be revealed. People will be judged not by their reputation but by their fruit.

This assurance is important, because discouragement can wreak havoc on your walk with Christ, especially as it relates to prayer. Discouraged people have a hard time staying consistent in their prayer time. Others become discouraged because they pray every day yet feel God has not answered a specific request. Discouragement can derail your prayer life if you are not careful.

EXPLORING THE TEXT

Jesus' Teaching on Prayer (Luke 11:1–13)

¹ Now it came to pass, as He was praying in a certain place, when He ceased, that one of His disciples said to Him, "Lord, teach us to pray, as John also taught his disciples."

² So He said to them, "When you pray, say:

Our Father in heaven,
Hallowed be Your name.
Your kingdom come.

Your will be done

On earth as it is in heaven.

³ Give us day by day our daily bread.

⁴ And forgive us our sins,

For we also forgive everyone who is indebted to us.

And do not lead us into temptation,

But deliver us from the evil one."

⁵ And He said to them, "Which of you shall have a friend, and go to him at midnight and say to him, 'Friend, lend me three loaves; ⁶ for a friend of mine has come to me on his journey, and I have nothing to set before him'; ⁷ and he will answer from within and say, 'Do not trouble me; the door is now shut, and my children are with me in bed; I cannot rise and give to you'? ⁸ I say to you, though he will not rise and give to him because he is his friend, yet because of his persistence he will rise and give him as many as he needs.

⁹ "So I say to you, ask, and it will be given to you; seek, and you will find; knock, and it will be opened to you. ¹⁰ For everyone who asks receives, and he who seeks finds, and to him who knocks it will be opened. ¹¹ If a son asks for bread from any father among you, will he give him a stone? Or if he asks for a fish, will he give him a serpent instead of a fish? ¹² Or if he asks for an egg, will he offer him a scorpion? ¹³ If you then, being evil, know how to give good gifts to your children, how much more will your heavenly Father give the Holy Spirit to those who ask Him!"

---

1. Why do you think Jesus taught His disciples to pray for bread on a *daily* basis instead of on a *weekly* or *monthly* basis (see verse 3)?

----

2. What does Jesus say about the importance of persisting in prayer (see verses 5–8)? Why do you think God asks us to continue to seek Him for the answers to our prayers?

_____

_____

_____

_____

Woe to the Pharisees and Experts in the Law (Luke 11:37–54)

37 And as He spoke, a certain Pharisee asked Him to dine with him. So He went in and sat down to eat. 38 When the Pharisee saw it, he marveled that He had not first washed before dinner.

39 Then the Lord said to him, "Now you Pharisees make the outside of the cup and dish clean, but your inward part is full of greed and wickedness. 40 Foolish ones! Did not He who made the outside make the inside also? 41 But rather give alms of such things as you have; then indeed all things are clean to you.

42 "But woe to you Pharisees! For you tithe mint and rue and all manner of herbs, and pass by justice and the love of God. These you ought to have done, without leaving the others undone. 43 Woe to you Pharisees! For you love the best seats in the synagogues and greetings in the marketplaces. 44 Woe to you, scribes and Pharisees, hypocrites! For you are like graves which are not seen, and the men who walk over them are not aware of them."

45 Then one of the lawyers answered and said to Him, "Teacher, by saying these things You reproach us also."

46 And He said, "Woe to you also, lawyers! For you load men with burdens hard to bear, and you yourselves do not touch the burdens with one of your fingers. 47 Woe to you! For you build the tombs of the prophets, and your fathers killed them. 48 In fact, you bear witness that you approve the deeds of your fathers; for they indeed killed

them, and you build their tombs. [49] Therefore the wisdom of God also said, 'I will send them prophets and apostles, and some of them they will kill and persecute,' [50] that the blood of all the prophets which was shed from the foundation of the world may be required of this generation, [51] from the blood of Abel to the blood of Zechariah who perished between the altar and the temple. Yes, I say to you, it shall be required of this generation.

[52] "Woe to you lawyers! For you have taken away the key of knowledge. You did not enter in yourselves, and those who were entering in you hindered."

[53] And as He said these things to them, the scribes and the Pharisees began to assail Him vehemently, and to cross-examine Him about many things, [54] lying in wait for Him, and seeking to catch Him in something He might say, that they might accuse Him.

---

3. What are some of the things Jesus accused the Pharisees and teachers of the law of doing . . . and *not* doing (see verses 42–44, 46–52)?

----

4. Jesus told the religious leaders, "You build the tombs of the prophets, and your fathers killed them" (verse 47). Read 1 Kings 18:4 and Matthew 14:1–12. Why do you think the Jewish people persecuted and killed God's prophets?

The Parable of the Rich Fool (Luke 12:13–34)

[13] Then one from the crowd said to Him, "Teacher, tell my brother to divide the inheritance with me."

[14] But He said to him, "Man, who made Me a judge or an arbitrator over you?" [15] And He said to them, "Take heed and beware of covetousness, for one's life does not consist in the abundance of the things he possesses."

[16] Then He spoke a parable to them, saying: "The ground of a certain rich man yielded plentifully. [17] And he thought within himself, saying, 'What shall I do, since I have no room to store my crops?' [18] So he said, 'I will do this: I will pull down my barns and build greater, and there I will store all my crops and my goods. [19] And I will say to my soul, "Soul, you have many goods laid up for many years; take your ease; eat, drink, and be merry." ' [20] But God said to him, 'Fool! This night your soul will be required of you; then whose will those things be which you have provided?'

[21] "So is he who lays up treasure for himself, and is not rich toward God."

[22] Then He said to His disciples, "Therefore I say to you, do not worry about your life, what you will eat; nor about the body, what you will put on. [23] Life is more than food, and the body is more than clothing. [24] Consider the ravens, for they neither sow nor reap, which have neither storehouse nor barn; and God feeds them. Of how much more value are you than the birds? [25] And which of you by worrying can add one cubit to his stature? [26] If you then are not able to do the least, why are you anxious for the rest? [27] Consider the lilies, how they grow: they neither toil nor spin; and yet I say to you, even Solomon in all his glory was not arrayed like one of these. [28] If then God so clothes the grass, which today is in the field and tomorrow is thrown into the oven, how much more will He clothe you, O you of little faith?

[29] "And do not seek what you should eat or what you should drink, nor have an anxious mind. [30] For all these things the nations

of the world seek after, and your Father knows that you need these things. ³¹ But seek the kingdom of God, and all these things shall be added to you.

³² "Do not fear, little flock, for it is your Father's good pleasure to give you the kingdom. ³³ Sell what you have and give alms; provide yourselves money bags which do not grow old, a treasure in the heavens that does not fail, where no thief approaches nor moth destroys. ³⁴ For where your treasure is, there your heart will be also."

---

5. The Jewish people in first-century Israel often consulted with rabbis to render a judgment in ethical and legal matters. But how did Jesus respond when someone asked Him to render a judgment in regard to splitting an inheritance (see verses 13–21)?

_____

_____

_____

_____

_____

6. What point was Jesus making when He asked His listeners to consider how God took care of the ravens and the lilies of the field (see verses 24–28)?

_____

_____

_____

_____

_____

_____

The Faithful Servant and the Evil Servant (Luke 12:35–53)

[35] "Let your waist be girded and your lamps burning; [36] and you yourselves be like men who wait for their master, when he will return from the wedding, that when he comes and knocks they may open to him immediately. [37] Blessed are those servants whom the master, when he comes, will find watching. Assuredly, I say to you that he will gird himself and have them sit down to eat, and will come and serve them. [38] And if he should come in the second watch, or come in the third watch, and find them so, blessed are those servants. [39] But know this, that if the master of the house had known what hour the thief would come, he would have watched and not allowed his house to be broken into. [40] Therefore you also be ready, for the Son of Man is coming at an hour you do not expect."

[41] Then Peter said to Him, "Lord, do You speak this parable only to us, or to all people?"

[42] And the Lord said, "Who then is that faithful and wise steward, whom his master will make ruler over his household, to give them their portion of food in due season? [43] Blessed is that servant whom his master will find so doing when he comes. [44] Truly, I say to you that he will make him ruler over all that he has. [45] But if that servant says in his heart, 'My master is delaying his coming,' and begins to beat the male and female servants, and to eat and drink and be drunk, [46] the master of that servant will come on a day when he is not looking for him, and at an hour when he is not aware, and will cut him in two and appoint him his portion with the unbelievers. [47] And that servant who knew his master's will, and did not prepare himself or do according to his will, shall be beaten with many stripes. [48] But he who did not know, yet committed things deserving of stripes, shall be beaten with few. For everyone to whom much is given, from him much will be required; and to whom much has been committed, of him they will ask the more.

[49] "I came to send fire on the earth, and how I wish it were already kindled! [50] But I have a baptism to be baptized with, and

how distressed I am till it is accomplished! [51] Do you suppose that I came to give peace on earth? I tell you, not at all, but rather division. [52] For from now on five in one house will be divided: three against two, and two against three. [53] Father will be divided against son and son against father, mother against daughter and daughter against mother, mother-in-law against her daughter-in-law and daughter-in-law against her mother-in-law."

---

7. What does Jesus promise to servants who are faithful to their Master (see verses 42–48)?

_____

_____

_____

_____

8. What kind of division did Jesus promise He would bring (see verses 49–53)? How might a person's decision to follow Christ cause strife and division within his or her household ?

_____

_____

_____

_____

REVIEWING THE STORY

Jesus understood just how damaging hypocrisy could be. After all, how could people trust a message was genuine if they couldn't trust the integrity of the messenger? Jesus thus urged His disciples to make wise decisions in the way they conducted themselves. He taught them to pray in a genuine way that pleased God. He pointed out the hypocrisy of the Jewish religious leaders. He urged His followers to obey God's word and not try to make a name for themselves in order to impress others, but instead to set a genuine example for the people in their world.

9. How does asking for God's "will to be done on earth" put a person in the right frame of mind for prayer (see Luke 11:2)?

_____

_____

_____

10. What was the motivation behind the Pharisees' and religious leaders' desire to be around Jesus and listen to His teachings (see Luke 11:53–54)?

_____

_____

_____

11. Why did Jesus instruct His disciples not to worry about the basic necessities of life, such as food and clothing? What were they to seek instead (see Luke 12:22–31)?

_____

_____

_____

12. What should followers of Jesus be doing as they wait for His return (see Luke 12:35–40)?

_____

_____

_____

APPLYING THE MESSAGE

13. What do you learn from Jesus' model prayer about what kinds of needs and requests to take to God? How does Jesus' example compare with the way you typically pray?

_____

_____

_____

14. Jesus said that He came "to send fire on the earth" (Luke 12:49). How have Jesus' teachings revolutionized your life? How has your relationship with Christ, or your obedience to a particular biblical teaching, caused division between you and a loved one?

_____

_____

_____

REFLECTING ON THE MEANING

Prayer is about _dependence_. When the disciples asked Jesus to teach them to pray, He told the story of a man who faced a need that he could not meet unless he got help from another source. If you are to learn to pray, you must realize that your circumstance is like that of this man. The reason prayer is hard for many people is that it involves recognizing that only God can make them all they ought to be.

Prayer is about _conflict_. It is a conflict of the will of the person who prays with what they anticipate is the will of the God to whom they pray. When you want something from your Father in heaven, you don't just _mention_ it to Him. Rather, you _barrage_ Him with persistent prayer. You knock on the door and keep knocking. You ask and keep asking. You seek and keep seeking. Prayer isn't passive but active. It's making the same request over and over again until God grants it or until He makes it clear that it's not His will for you.

Prayer is a *challenge*, especially when it seems as though God isn't listening. When you receive no answer, you must continue praying. You must not judge your prayers based on what you see happening or don't see happening. Sometimes, God may delay His answer in order to give you more than you requested. As Jesus said to His disciples, "If you then, being evil, know how to give good gifts to your children, how much more will your heavenly Father give the Holy Spirit to those who ask Him!" (Luke 11:13).

The greatest blessing of prayer lies not in receiving the answer but in being the kind of person God can trust with the answer. If you take God at His word, believe that prayer changes things, pray without ceasing, and keep asking, knocking, and seeking, there will come a time when He will say, "I will answer your prayer because you can handle the answer."

JOURNALING YOUR RESPONSE

What is the biggest obstacle that hinders your prayer life from being what it could be?

COUNT THE COST

Luke 13:1–14:35

GETTING STARTED

What are some things that you have had to leave behind to follow Jesus?

_____

_____

_____

_____

_____

_____

_____

_____

SETTING THE STAGE

In Luke 13 and 14, Jesus established a protocol for those who would follow Him. He called people to *repent*—which means to not only ask forgiveness for their sins but also to turn from their sinful ways. He emphasized the importance of listening to the Word of God and of bearing fruit. He wanted His disciples to show through their actions that the Word was having an impact on their lives and something productive was happening within them.

The Pharisees and other religious leaders stood in stark contrast to these repentant disciples who approached God's Word with a humble spirit and an eagerness to learn. Blinded by their pride, and convinced they were experts in Scripture, they used God's law as a weapon to make other people feel inferior, inadequate, and hopeless. At least . . . they *tried* to do so. Even as they continued their attempts to thwart Jesus' ministry, He persisted in shutting them down by exposing their hypocrisy for everyone to see.

Jesus continued to challenge His followers by communicating eternal truths through stories the Pharisees couldn't interpret. He also revealed the extent of the faithfulness He expected from His followers. The life that Jesus called them to lead would not be an easy one. In fact, as we have seen, it would put them at odds with family and friends. This life would require them to turn their backs on things they had once enjoyed—even things that were an integral part of their lives. It would take them to places where they would be uncomfortable, not to mention places where their safety and well-being were not necessarily guaranteed.

But, in the end, Jesus promised His followers that it would all be worth it.

EXPLORING THE TEXT

Repent or Perish (Luke 13:1–17)

> [1] There were present at that season some who told Him about the Galileans whose blood Pilate had mingled with their sacrifices. [2] And Jesus answered and said to them, "Do you suppose that these Galileans were worse sinners than all other Galileans, because they suffered such things? [3] I tell you, no; but unless you repent you will all likewise perish. [4] Or those eighteen on whom the tower in Siloam fell and killed them, do you think that they were worse sinners than all other men who dwelt in Jerusalem? [5] I tell you, no; but unless you repent you will all likewise perish."
>
> [6] He also spoke this parable: "A certain man had a fig tree planted in his vineyard, and he came seeking fruit on it and found none. [7] Then he said to the keeper of his vineyard, 'Look, for three years I have

come seeking fruit on this fig tree and find none. Cut it down; why does it use up the ground?' ⁸ But he answered and said to him, 'Sir, let it alone this year also, until I dig around it and fertilize it. ⁹ And if it bears fruit, well. But if not, after that you can cut it down.' "

¹⁰ Now He was teaching in one of the synagogues on the Sabbath. ¹¹ And behold, there was a woman who had a spirit of infirmity eighteen years, and was bent over and could in no way raise herself up. ¹² But when Jesus saw her, He called her to Him and said to her, "Woman, you are loosed from your infirmity." ¹³ And He laid His hands on her, and immediately she was made straight, and glorified God.

¹⁴ But the ruler of the synagogue answered with indignation, because Jesus had healed on the Sabbath; and he said to the crowd, "There are six days on which men ought to work; therefore come and be healed on them, and not on the Sabbath day."

¹⁵ The Lord then answered him and said, "Hypocrite! Does not each one of you on the Sabbath loose his ox or donkey from the stall, and lead it away to water it? ¹⁶ So ought not this woman, being a daughter of Abraham, whom Satan has bound—think of it—for eighteen years, be loosed from this bond on the Sabbath?" ¹⁷ And when He said these things, all His adversaries were put to shame; and all the multitude rejoiced for all the glorious things that were done by Him.

---

1. The Jewish people—and even Jesus' own disciples—were often quick to associate a tragedy in a person's life with that person's sin (see John 9:1–2). How does Jesus respond to that particular way of thinking in this passage (see Luke 13:1–5)?

----

2. Jesus expected His followers to be productive members of the kingdom of God (see verses 6–9). How did the ruler of the synagogue reveal himself to be "unproductive" when he criticized Jesus for healing a woman on the Sabbath (see verses 14–16)?

The Narrow Gate (Luke 13:18–30)

[18] Then He said, "What is the kingdom of God like? And to what shall I compare it? [19] It is like a mustard seed, which a man took and put in his garden; and it grew and became a large tree, and the birds of the air nested in its branches."

[20] And again He said, "To what shall I liken the kingdom of God? [21] It is like leaven, which a woman took and hid in three measures of meal till it was all leavened."

[22] And He went through the cities and villages, teaching, and journeying toward Jerusalem. [23] Then one said to Him, "Lord, are there few who are saved?"

And He said to them, [24] "Strive to enter through the narrow gate, for many, I say to you, will seek to enter and will not be able. [25] When once the Master of the house has risen up and shut the door, and you begin to stand outside and knock at the door, saying, 'Lord, Lord, open for us,' and He will answer and say to you, 'I do not know you, where you are from,' [26] then you will begin to say, 'We ate and drank in Your presence, and You taught in our streets.' [27] But He will say, 'I tell you I do not know you, where you are from. Depart from Me, all you workers of iniquity.' [28] There will be weeping and gnashing of teeth, when you see Abraham and Isaac and Jacob and all the prophets in the kingdom of God, and yourselves thrust out. [29] They will come from the east and the west, from the north and the south, and sit down in the kingdom of God. ³⁰ And indeed there are last who will be first, and there are first who will be last."

---

3. The Jews in the first century expected the Messiah to arrive as a conquering hero, establishing a dominant political kingdom on the earth. How does that expectation compare with the way Jesus described the kingdom of God (see verses 18–20)?

4. The rabbis of Jesus' day differed in their opinions as to whether a great or small number of people would receive salvation in God's kingdom. How did Jesus choose to answer this question? According to Jesus, who will receive God's salvation? Who won't (see verses 24–28)?

Take the Lowly Place (Luke 14:1–14)

¹ Now it happened, as He went into the house of one of the rulers of the Pharisees to eat bread on the Sabbath, that they watched Him closely. ² And behold, there was a certain man before Him who had dropsy. ³ And Jesus, answering, spoke to the lawyers and Pharisees, saying, "Is it lawful to heal on the Sabbath?"

⁴ But they kept silent. And He took him and healed him, and let him go. ⁵ Then He answered them, saying, "Which of you, having a donkey or an ox that has fallen into a pit, will not immediately pull him out on the Sabbath day?" ⁶ And they could not answer Him regarding these things.

⁷ So He told a parable to those who were invited, when He noted how they chose the best places, saying to them: ⁸ "When you are invited by anyone to a wedding feast, do not sit down in the best place, lest one more honorable than you be invited by him; ⁹ and he who invited you and him come and say to you, 'Give place to this man,' and then you begin with shame to take the lowest place. ¹⁰ But when you are invited, go and sit down in the lowest place, so that when he who invited you comes he may say to you, 'Friend, go up higher.' Then you will have glory in the presence of those who sit at the table with you. ¹¹ For whoever exalts himself will be humbled, and he who humbles himself will be exalted."

¹² Then He also said to him who invited Him, "When you give a dinner or a supper, do not ask your friends, your brothers, your relatives, nor rich neighbors, lest they also invite you back, and you be repaid. ¹³ But when you give a feast, invite the poor, the maimed, the lame, the blind. ¹⁴ And you will be blessed, because they cannot repay you; for you shall be repaid at the resurrection of the just."

---

5. Jesus knew the Pharisees were trying to find fault with Him. Why do you think He accepted an invitation to eat at the house of one of the rulers of the Pharisees (see verse 1)?

6. Two of the Pharisees' favorite pastimes were being noticed and making themselves look important. How do you think they responded to Jesus' parable about being invited to a wedding feast (see verses 7–11)?

_____

_____

_____

_____

_____

_____

_____

The Parable of the Great Banquet (Luke 14:15–33)

15 Now when one of those who sat at the table with Him heard these things, he said to Him, "Blessed is he who shall eat bread in the kingdom of God!"

16 Then He said to him, "A certain man gave a great supper and invited many, 17 and sent his servant at supper time to say to those who were invited, 'Come, for all things are now ready.' 18 But they all with one accord began to make excuses. The first said to him, 'I have bought a piece of ground, and I must go and see it. I ask you to have me excused.' 19 And another said, 'I have bought five yoke of oxen, and I am going to test them. I ask you to have me excused.' 20 Still another said, 'I have married a wife, and therefore I cannot come.' 21 So that servant came and reported these things to his master. Then the master of the house, being angry, said to his servant, 'Go out quickly into the streets and lanes of the city, and bring in here the poor and the maimed and the lame and the blind.' 22 And the servant said, 'Master, it is done as you commanded, and still there is room.' 23 Then the master said to the servant, 'Go out into the highways and hedges, and compel them to come in, that my house may be filled. 24 For I say to you that none of those men who were invited shall taste my supper.' "

²⁵ Now great multitudes went with Him. And He turned and said to them, ²⁶ "If anyone comes to Me and does not hate his father and mother, wife and children, brothers and sisters, yes, and his own life also, he cannot be My disciple. ²⁷ And whoever does not bear his cross and come after Me cannot be My disciple. ²⁸ For which of you, intending to build a tower, does not sit down first and count the cost, whether he has enough to finish it— ²⁹ lest, after he has laid the foundation, and is not able to finish, all who see it begin to mock him, ³⁰ saying, 'This man began to build and was not able to finish'? ³¹ Or what king, going to make war against another king, does not sit down first and consider whether he is able with ten thousand to meet him who comes against him with twenty thousand? ³² Or else, while the other is still a great way off, he sends a delegation and asks conditions of peace. ³³ So likewise, whoever of you does not forsake all that he has cannot be My disciple."

---

7. In the parable of the great banquet, what are some of the reasons the people gave for turning down the host's invitation? What did the host do when he received this response (see verses 18–24)?

_____

_____

_____

_____

8. What did Jesus say were some of the costs of following Him (see verses 26–33)?

_____

_____

_____

_____

REVIEWING THE STORY

Compassion is one of the many traits that set Jesus apart from the Jewish religious leaders of His day. The Pharisees and teachers of the law cared little about the people's suffering or need. They were too busy trying to enforce their regulations about what someone could and could not do on the Sabbath. Jesus ignored their manmade rules by performing various healings on the Sabbath . . . right in front of the Pharisees. He then exposed the hypocrisy of those who opposed Him and spoke using parables they could not understand.

9. God created the Sabbath for the benefit of people. In His compassion, He gave us a day set apart for rest, relaxation, and recharging. What might it have been like on the Sabbath for a normal Jewish person living under the scrutiny of the Pharisees (see Luke 13:14)?

_____

_____

_____

_____

_____

10. Jesus said to the religious leaders, "I am the door. If anyone enters by Me, he will be saved, and will go in and out and find pasture" (John 10:9). Given this context, what does it mean to take the "narrow gate" when it comes to following Christ (see Luke 13:24)?

_____

_____

_____

_____

_____

11. What attitudes and actions did Jesus commend when it came to being "exalted" in God's kingdom (see Luke 14:7–14)?

_____

_____

_____

_____

_____

_____

12. What does the parable of the man building the tower reveal about the need to consider the cost of truly committing your life to Christ (see Luke 14:28–31)?

_____

_____

_____

_____

_____

APPLYING THE MESSAGE

13. Repentance is more than just asking forgiveness—it's turning completely away from your old lifestyle and starting a new one. Why do you think this is so difficult?

_____

_____

_____

_____

_____

14. What have you discovered about the cost of following Christ? What have you *gained* from following Him?

_____

_____

_____

_____

_____

REFLECTING ON THE MEANING

Jesus' clash with the Pharisees highlights a surprising truth. Following rules is a lot easier than following Christ. The Pharisees were all about rules. They drew lines and made their home within them. They created dozens of regulations as to what they could and could not do in any given situation. Their lives were about following those regulations to the letter of the law. In their way of thinking, the better rule-follower you were, the more righteous you were.

Peter tried to draw similar lines of reasoning when he asked Jesus how many times he was expected to forgive someone who had wronged him (see Matthew 18:21). He probably thought he was being magnanimous when he suggested *seven* times. But it was still a line . . . a matter of accounting. The motive behind Peter's question was to establish a guideline—a point at which his responsibility to forgive the other person would end.

Jesus erased those lines. He stressed the life that He was calling His followers to lead couldn't be structured by a list of rules and regulations. It was messier and more complicated because it involved *love*—genuine, humble, sacrificial love for God and for others. While those who adhered to the Jewish Law were concerned with obeying the rules of the Sabbath, those who adhered to God's law of love were concerned with those who were hurting on the Sabbath. As Jesus' followers, we do not have the option of hiding behind rules and regulations. We are called to ease the pain of the hurting in the world and meet the needs of those who are ignored by others.

There is nothing easy about Jesus' call because people are messy—they are complicated, stubborn, proud, prejudiced, ungrateful, and unpredictable. That goes for the people in need as well as for the Christians trying to help them! Still, it is Jesus' will for us to love others . . . and where there's His will, there's a way. He blesses and multiplies our efforts as we "get our hands dirty" by working in the lives of those in need.

JOURNALING YOUR RESPONSE

Who needs you the most right now? What would Jesus have you do in that person's life?

LOST AND FOUND

Luke 15:1–16:31

GETTING STARTED

What's the most precious or valuable thing you've ever lost? What did you do to try to find it?

_____

_____

_____

_____

_____

_____

_____

_____

_____

_____

_____

_____

SETTING THE STAGE

In Luke 15, Jesus tells three stories, which are really part of one parable. The first is the story of a lost sheep. The second is the story of a lost coin. The third is the story of a lost son. In the progression of these stories, the object being sought becomes increasingly more precious. The lost sheep is one of one hundred. The lost coin is one of ten. The lost son is one of two. In all of these stories, Jesus is the person who is seeking that which is lost. He is the shepherd, He is the one looking for the coin, and He is the father looking for the lost son.

Jesus never told a story without having a reason behind it. His purpose in telling this three-part parable can be found in Luke 15:1–2. The scribes and Pharisees were watching Jesus as He spent time with tax collectors, outcasts, and other undesirables. What they saw caused them to grumble, "This man receives sinners and eats with them."

Jesus addressed their complaint by saying, in effect, "Sit down. Let Me tell you a few stories. You're absolutely right. I do receive sinners, and I do eat with them. But you don't take it far enough. I run after sinners! I run out to the village to greet them. I go into their smug self-centeredness and plead with them to come in. I'm all about sinners because My mission is this: 'The Son of Man has come to seek and to save that which was lost'" (Matthew 18:11).

Jesus told the stories to help the Pharisees understand that His whole purpose in life was the very thing of which they were accusing Him: reaching out with His grace to sinners.

EXPLORING THE TEXT

The Lost Sheep and Lost Coin (Luke 15:1–10)

---

¹ Then all the tax collectors and the sinners drew near to Him to hear Him. ² And the Pharisees and scribes complained, saying, "This Man receives sinners and eats with them." ³ So He spoke this parable to them, saying:

⁴ "What man of you, having a hundred sheep, if he loses one of them, does not leave the ninety-nine in the wilderness, and go after the one which is lost until he finds it? ⁵ And when he has found it, he lays it on his shoulders, rejoicing. ⁶ And when he comes home,

he calls together his friends and neighbors, saying to them, 'Rejoice with me, for I have found my sheep which was lost!' ⁷ I say to you that likewise there will be more joy in heaven over one sinner who repents than over ninety-nine just persons who need no repentance.

⁸ "Or what woman, having ten silver coins, if she loses one coin, does not light a lamp, sweep the house, and search carefully until she finds it? ⁹ And when she has found it, she calls her friends and neighbors together, saying, 'Rejoice with me, for I have found the piece which I lost!' ¹⁰ Likewise, I say to you, there is joy in the presence of the angels of God over one sinner who repents."

---

1. What complaint did the Pharisees and scribes lodge against Jesus (see verses 1–2)?

_____

_____

_____

_____

_____

2. How did Jesus answer their accusation? How did the stories He told communicate the purpose of His mission to the Pharisees and scribes (see verses 4–10)?

_____

_____

_____

_____

_____

_____

_____

The Parable of the Two Sons (Luke 15:11–32)

11 Then He said: "A certain man had two sons. 12 And the younger of them said to his father, 'Father, give me the portion of goods that falls to me.' So he divided to them his livelihood. 13 And not many days after, the younger son gathered all together, journeyed to a far country, and there wasted his possessions with prodigal living. 14 But when he had spent all, there arose a severe famine in that land, and he began to be in want. 15 Then he went and joined himself to a citizen of that country, and he sent him into his fields to feed swine. 16 And he would gladly have filled his stomach with the pods that the swine ate, and no one gave him anything."

17 "But when he came to himself, he said, 'How many of my father's hired servants have bread enough and to spare, and I perish with hunger! 18 I will arise and go to my father, and will say to him, 'Father, I have sinned against heaven and before you, 19 and I am no longer worthy to be called your son. Make me like one of your hired servants.' "

20 "And he arose and came to his father. But when he was still a great way off, his father saw him and had compassion, and ran and fell on his neck and kissed him. 21 And the son said to him, 'Father, I have sinned against heaven and in your sight, and am no longer worthy to be called your son.'"

22 "But the father said to his servants, 'Bring out the best robe and put it on him, and put a ring on his hand and sandals on his feet. 23 And bring the fatted calf here and kill it, and let us eat and be merry; 24 for this my son was dead and is alive again; he was lost and is found.' And they began to be merry."

25 "Now his older son was in the field. And as he came and drew near to the house, he heard music and dancing. 26 So he called one of the servants and asked what these things meant. 27 And he said to him, 'Your brother has come, and because he has received him safe and sound, your father has killed the fatted calf.' "

²⁸ "But he was angry and would not go in. Therefore his father came out and pleaded with him. ²⁹ So he answered and said to his father, 'Lo, these many years I have been serving you; I never transgressed your commandment at any time; and yet you never gave me a young goat, that I might make merry with my friends. ³⁰ But as soon as this son of yours came, who has devoured your livelihood with harlots, you killed the fatted calf for him.' "

³¹ "And he said to him, 'Son, you are always with me, and all that I have is yours. ³² It was right that we should make merry and be glad, for your brother was dead and is alive again, and was lost and is found.' "

---

3. What were some of the ways the younger son brought shame to his father and his family? What kind of "sinner" does he represent (see verses 11–16)?

_____

_____

_____

_____

_____

_____

4. What was the older brother's attitude toward his younger brother and his father? What type of "sinner" does he represent (see verses 25–30)?

_____

_____

_____

_____

_____

The Parable of the Unjust Steward (Luke 16:1–13)

[1] He also said to His disciples: "There was a certain rich man who had a steward, and an accusation was brought to him that this man was wasting his goods. [2] So he called him and said to him, 'What is this I hear about you? Give an account of your stewardship, for you can no longer be steward.'

[3] "Then the steward said within himself, 'What shall I do? For my master is taking the stewardship away from me. I cannot dig; I am ashamed to beg. [4] I have resolved what to do, that when I am put out of the stewardship, they may receive me into their houses.'

[5] "So he called every one of his master's debtors to him, and said to the first, 'How much do you owe my master?' [6] And he said, 'A hundred measures of oil.' So he said to him, 'Take your bill, and sit down quickly and write fifty.' [7] Then he said to another, 'And how much do you owe?' So he said, 'A hundred measures of wheat.' And he said to him, 'Take your bill, and write eighty.' [8] So the master commended the unjust steward because he had dealt shrewdly. For the sons of this world are more shrewd in their generation than the sons of light.

[9] "And I say to you, make friends for yourselves by unrighteous mammon, that when you fail, they may receive you into an everlasting home. [10] He who is faithful in what is least is faithful also in much; and he who is unjust in what is least is unjust also in much. [11] Therefore if you have not been faithful in the unrighteous mammon, who will commit to your trust the true riches? [12] And if you have not been faithful in what is another man's, who will give you what is your own?

[13] "No servant can serve two masters; for either he will hate the one and love the other, or else he will be loyal to the one and despise the other. You cannot serve God and mammon."

5. How did the master respond to the steward's actions? What point do you think Jesus was making by telling this parable (see verses 1–8)?

_____

_____

_____

_____

_____

6. For what purpose did Jesus say His followers should use their worldly wealth? What is the relationship between loving/serving money and loving/serving God (see verses 9–13)?

_____

_____

_____

_____

_____

The Rich Man and Lazarus (Luke 16:19–31)

¹⁹ There was a certain rich man who was clothed in purple and fine linen and fared sumptuously every day. ²⁰ But there was a certain beggar named Lazarus, full of sores, who was laid at his gate, ²¹ desiring to be fed with the crumbs which fell from the rich man's table. Moreover the dogs came and licked his sores. ²² So it was that the beggar died, and was carried by the angels to Abraham's bosom. The rich man also died and was buried. ²³ And being in torments in Hades, he lifted up his eyes and saw Abraham afar off, and Lazarus in his bosom.

²⁴ "Then he cried and said, 'Father Abraham, have mercy on me, and send Lazarus that he may dip the tip of his finger in water and

cool my tongue; for I am tormented in this flame.' [25] But Abraham said, 'Son, remember that in your lifetime you received your good things, and likewise Lazarus evil things; but now he is comforted and you are tormented. [26] And besides all this, between us and you there is a great gulf fixed, so that those who want to pass from here to you cannot, nor can those from there pass to us.'

[27] "Then he said, 'I beg you therefore, father, that you would send him to my father's house, [28] for I have five brothers, that he may testify to them, lest they also come to this place of torment.' [29] Abraham said to him, 'They have Moses and the prophets; let them hear them.' [30] And he said, 'No, father Abraham; but if one goes to them from the dead, they will repent.' [31] But he said to him, 'If they do not hear Moses and the prophets, neither will they be persuaded though one rise from the dead.' "

---

7. How does Jesus depict the two men at the beginning of His parable (see verses 19–21)?

_____

_____

_____

_____

_____

8. What requests did the rich man make of Abraham? Why did Abraham refuse to grant these requests (see verses 24–31)?

_____

_____

_____

_____

_____

REVIEWING THE STORY

Jesus told many parables to explain how God desires all who are spiritually lost to be found in Him. In one story, He depicted God as a shepherd who left ninety-nine sheep behind to go in search of one that is lost. In another story, He depicted God as a woman who searched every inch of her house until she found a lost coin. He told of a story of two sons to show how God is a loving father who is always eager and ready to take His prodigal children back into His family. Jesus urged His followers (through the parable of the unjust steward) to use their earthly resources to gain lost souls and he warned His followers (through the parable of the rich man and Lazarus) of the consequences for *not* reaching out to the lost. Jesus wanted His followers to understand the time was short in reaching the world with the gospel.

9. How did the shepherd and the woman respond when they lost something important to them? How did they react when they found what was lost (see Luke 15:4–9)?

10. What makes the father a truly remarkable character in the parable of the two sons (see Luke 15:20–24, 29–31)?

11. What did Jesus mean when He said, "No servant can serve two masters" (Luke 16:13)? What is the danger of people making the pursuit of wealth a top priority in their lives?

_____

_____

_____

_____

12. In Jesus' parable of the rich man and Lazarus, "Moses and the prophets" refers to Scripture. Why do you think the rich man and his brothers rejected God's Word (see Luke 16:29–31)?

_____

_____

_____

_____

APPLYING THE MESSAGE

13. What are some of the ways that you are using your resources to reach the lost with the message and hope of Christ?

_____

_____

_____

_____

14. What is your reaction when you picture the rich man in Hades, begging Abraham to send someone to share the truth about eternity with his brothers?

_____

_____

_____

_____

REFLECTING ON THE MEANING

The loss Jesus describes in his trio of parables is no small matter. The man who lost one of his sheep still had ninety-nine others. Yet he searched the wilderness until he found the missing sheep, carried it home on his shoulders, and then called his friends and neighbors to tell them the news so they could celebrate with him. The woman who lost a silver coin still had nine others. Yet she lit a lamp, swept her entire house, and searched everywhere until she found it. She, too, called her friends and neighbors so they could share in her celebration.

The father of the prodigal son ignored the cultural rules of decorum and propriety in his search for his son. The younger son, by insisting on his share of the inheritance, had basically told the father that he no longer wanted to be a part of his family. But the father watched and waited for his lost son's return, and when he saw him off in the distance, he broke social norms by actually running to meet him. When the father found the son, he celebrated his return to the family with an enormous feast.

The two most important features these parables share in common are a sense of urgency when something (or someone) is lost and an unbridled celebration when something (or someone) is found. Having God's sense of urgency for the spiritual well-being of others means *recognizing tomorrow is promised to no one*. We never know when an opportunity to share our faith might be our last. We all know people who are lost. The question is how their condition affects us . . . and how we will seize the opportunity to share our faith when it arises.

Celebrating when someone who is lost is found means having the *same compassion Jesus had for people* and the same desire to see them come into God's kingdom. Jesus said, "There will be more joy in heaven over one sinner who repents than over ninety-nine just persons who need no repentance" (Luke 15:7). If you embrace this same mindset on earth, you may become a source of much-needed encouragement for the people around you.

Journaling Your Response

Who celebrated your decision to become a Christian?

ENCOUNTERS WITH JESUS

Luke 17:1–18:43

GETTING STARTED

Imagine that you get word that Jesus is passing through your town. You have one chance to see Him and make a request of Him. What would you say?

_____

_____

_____

_____

_____

_____

_____

_____

SETTING THE STAGE

The actual words of Jesus, which are marked in red in some Bibles, are rare and precious. Of the sixty-six books in the Bible, only four—the Gospels of Matthew, Mark, Luke, and John—contain the bulk of Jesus' recorded words. (Other books, including Acts and Revelation, record a few quotations of Christ here and there.)

Even in the Gospels, Jesus' words make up only a small percentage of the total text of the books. If His words were cut and pasted together, they would run only a few chapters long. What is surprising, as we have seen, is that a significant percentage of those words are wrapped up in parables. This raises the question as to *why* Jesus used so many stories. Why didn't He just give His followers instructions about how to live using easy-to-understand language?

The short answer is that Jesus understood that parables—or what we might call "word pictures"—are the most powerful means of human communication apart from drama or reenactment. It's no wonder that Jesus was a master storyteller. He had truth He wanted to deposit in the hearts of people so they would never forget His message.

If someone told you that Jesus was opposed to showy religion, the words probably wouldn't register, at least not for very long. But if someone told you a story that Jesus told, you wouldn't be able to forget it. Luke tells us that Jesus told stories to certain individuals "who trusted in themselves that they were righteous, and despised others" (18:9). He could have walked up to those people and said, "Stop trusting in yourselves and stop despising others." That would have been the direct route. But Jesus didn't do that. Instead, He told a story.

EXPLORING THE TEXT

Faith and Gratitude (Luke 17:1–19)

---

¹ Then He said to the disciples, "It is impossible that no offenses should come, but woe to him through whom they do come! ² It would be better for him if a millstone were hung around his neck, and he were thrown into the sea, than that he should offend one of these little ones. ³ Take heed to yourselves. If your brother sins against you, rebuke him; and if he repents, forgive him. ⁴ And if he sins against you seven times in a day, and seven times in a day returns to you, saying, 'I repent,' you shall forgive him."

⁵ And the apostles said to the Lord, "Increase our faith."

⁶ So the Lord said, "If you have faith as a mustard seed, you can say to this mulberry tree, 'Be pulled up by the roots and be planted in

the sea,' and it would obey you. [7] And which of you, having a servant plowing or tending sheep, will say to him when he has come in from the field, 'Come at once and sit down to eat'? [8] But will he not rather say to him, 'Prepare something for my supper, and gird yourself and serve me till I have eaten and drunk, and afterward you will eat and drink'? [9] Does he thank that servant because he did the things that were commanded him? I think not. [10] So likewise you, when you have done all those things which you are commanded, say, 'We are unprofitable servants. We have done what was our duty to do.' "

[11] Now it happened as He went to Jerusalem that He passed through the midst of Samaria and Galilee. [12] Then as He entered a certain village, there met Him ten men who were lepers, who stood afar off. [13] And they lifted up their voices and said, "Jesus, Master, have mercy on us!"

[14] So when He saw them, He said to them, "Go, show yourselves to the priests." And so it was that as they went, they were cleansed.

[15] And one of them, when he saw that he was healed, returned, and with a loud voice glorified God, [16] and fell down on his face at His feet, giving Him thanks. And he was a Samaritan.

[17] So Jesus answered and said, "Were there not ten cleansed? But where are the nine? [18] Were there not any found who returned to give glory to God except this foreigner?" [19] And He said to him, "Arise, go your way. Your faith has made you well."

---

1. What does Jesus say about the power of faith? What does the parable of the master and his servants say about what our motivations should be for serving others (see verses 6–10)?

_____

_____

_____

_____

_____

2. Aside from the man's overwhelming sense of gratitude, what were the differences between the leper who returned to thank Jesus and the nine who did not (see verses 15–19)?

_____

_____

_____

_____

_____

_____

_____

The Coming of the Kingdom (Luke 17:20–37)

20 Now when He was asked by the Pharisees when the kingdom of God would come, He answered them and said, "The kingdom of God does not come with observation; 21 nor will they say, 'See here!' or 'See there!' For indeed, the kingdom of God is within you."

22 Then He said to the disciples, "The days will come when you will desire to see one of the days of the Son of Man, and you will not see it. 23 And they will say to you, 'Look here!' or 'Look there!' Do not go after them or follow them. 24 For as the lightning that flashes out of one part under heaven shines to the other part under heaven, so also the Son of Man will be in His day. 25 But first He must suffer many things and be rejected by this generation. 26 And as it was in the days of Noah, so it will be also in the days of the Son of Man: 27 They ate, they drank, they married wives, they were given in marriage, until the day that Noah entered the ark, and the flood came and destroyed them all. 28 Likewise as it was also in the days of Lot: They ate, they drank, they bought, they sold, they planted, they built; 29 but on the day that Lot went out of Sodom it rained fire and brimstone from heaven and destroyed them all. 30 Even so will it be in the day when the Son of Man is revealed.

³¹ "In that day, he who is on the housetop, and his goods are in the house, let him not come down to take them away. And likewise the one who is in the field, let him not turn back. ³² Remember Lot's wife. ³³ Whoever seeks to save his life will lose it, and whoever loses his life will preserve it. ³⁴ I tell you, in that night there will be two men in one bed: the one will be taken and the other will be left. ³⁵ Two women will be grinding together: the one will be taken and the other left. ³⁶ Two men will be in the field: the one will be taken and the other left."

³⁷ And they answered and said to Him, "Where, Lord?"

So He said to them, "Wherever the body is, there the eagles will be gathered together."

---

3. What was the Pharisees' confusion about the kingdom of God (see verses 20–21)?

_____

_____

_____

_____

_____

4. What do Jesus' references to the days of Noah and Lot say about the situation that will be on earth when the Son of Man returns (see verses 26–30)?

_____

_____

_____

_____

_____

_____

Parables on Prayer (Luke 18:1–17)

¹ Then He spoke a parable to them, that men always ought to pray and not lose heart, ² saying: "There was in a certain city a judge who did not fear God nor regard man. ³ Now there was a widow in that city; and she came to him, saying, 'Get justice for me from my adversary.' ⁴ And he would not for a while; but afterward he said within himself, 'Though I do not fear God nor regard man, ⁵ yet because this widow troubles me I will avenge her, lest by her continual coming she weary me.' "

⁶ Then the Lord said, "Hear what the unjust judge said. ⁷ And shall God not avenge His own elect who cry out day and night to Him, though He bears long with them? ⁸ I tell you that He will avenge them speedily. Nevertheless, when the Son of Man comes, will He really find faith on the earth?"

⁹ Also He spoke this parable to some who trusted in themselves that they were righteous, and despised others: ¹⁰ "Two men went up to the temple to pray, one a Pharisee and the other a tax collector. ¹¹ The Pharisee stood and prayed thus with himself, 'God, I thank You that I am not like other men—extortioners, unjust, adulterers, or even as this tax collector. ¹² I fast twice a week; I give tithes of all that I possess.' ¹³ And the tax collector, standing afar off, would not so much as raise his eyes to heaven, but beat his breast, saying, 'God, be merciful to me a sinner!' ¹⁴ I tell you, this man went down to his house justified rather than the other; for everyone who exalts himself will be humbled, and he who humbles himself will be exalted."

¹⁵ Then they also brought infants to Him that He might touch them; but when the disciples saw it, they rebuked them. ¹⁶ But Jesus called them to Him and said, "Let the little children come to Me, and do not forbid them; for of such is the kingdom of God. ¹⁷ Assuredly, I say to you, whoever does not receive the kingdom of God as a little child will by no means enter it."

5. Why did the judge ultimately agree to answer the widow's request? What point was Jesus making with this parable about approaching God in prayer (see verses 3–8)?

_____

_____

_____

_____

_____

6. What were the differences between the prayer of the Pharisee and the prayer of the tax collector (see verses 9–14)?

_____

_____

_____

_____

_____

The Rich Young Ruler (Luke 18:18–34)

18 Now a certain ruler asked Him, saying, "Good Teacher, what shall I do to inherit eternal life?"

19 So Jesus said to him, "Why do you call Me good? No one is good but One, that is, God. 20 You know the commandments: 'Do not commit adultery,' 'Do not murder,' 'Do not steal,' 'Do not bear false witness,' 'Honor your father and your mother.' "

21 And he said, "All these things I have kept from my youth."

22 So when Jesus heard these things, He said to him, "You still lack one thing. Sell all that you have and distribute to the poor, and you will have treasure in heaven; and come, follow Me."

23 But when he heard this, he became very sorrowful, for he was very rich.

²⁴ And when Jesus saw that he became very sorrowful, He said, "How hard it is for those who have riches to enter the kingdom of God! ²⁵ For it is easier for a camel to go through the eye of a needle than for a rich man to enter the kingdom of God."

²⁶ And those who heard it said, "Who then can be saved?"

²⁷ But He said, "The things which are impossible with men are possible with God."

²⁸ Then Peter said, "See, we have left all and followed You."

²⁹ So He said to them, "Assuredly, I say to you, there is no one who has left house or parents or brothers or wife or children, for the sake of the kingdom of God, ³⁰ who shall not receive many times more in this present time, and in the age to come eternal life."

³¹ Then He took the twelve aside and said to them, "Behold, we are going up to Jerusalem, and all things that are written by the prophets concerning the Son of Man will be accomplished. ³² For He will be delivered to the Gentiles and will be mocked and insulted and spit upon. ³³ They will scourge Him and kill Him. And the third day He will rise again."

³⁴ But they understood none of these things; this saying was hidden from them, and they did not know the things which were spoken.

---

7. Jesus had previously said, "No servant can serve two masters . . . you cannot serve God and mammon" (Luke 16:13). What was Jesus really asking the young ruler to do when He instructed him to sell his possessions and give the money to the poor (see Luke 18:22)?

_____

_____

_____

_____

_____

8. What did Jesus promise to Peter and all disciples who sacrifice for God's kingdom (see verses 28–30)?

_____

_____

_____

_____

_____

_____

REVIEWING THE STORY

Jesus often spoke with His followers about the nature of God's kingdom and the power they had been given as members of it. In one teaching, He emphasized how if they had faith even the size of "a mustard seed," they had the authority in prayer to command a mulberry tree to be uprooted and planted in the sea. He told His followers the days would be difficult as they waited for the fulfillment of God's kingdom on earth, but as they waited they should be persisting in prayer—just like the widow who persisted in pressing her case to a judge. Jesus also stressed those who seek to "save their lives" by following their own paths will only end up losing everything. This was the case for the young ruler, who wanted eternal life but could not let go of his riches.

9. How did Jesus reply to the disciples' request for Him to increase their faith (see Luke 17:6)?

_____

_____

_____

_____

_____

_____

10. Why did Jesus indicate that His followers needed to be continually waiting and watching for His return (see Luke 17:31–36)?

_____

_____

_____

_____

11. What types of attitudes does God want a person to have when approaching Him in prayer (see Luke 18:9–17)?

_____

_____

_____

_____

12. The ruler who came to Jesus in search of eternal life is one of the few people in the Gospels who left Jesus' presence feeling sadder than when he arrived. Why was he sorrowful when he walked away from his encounter with Christ (see Luke 18:18–23)?

_____

_____

_____

_____

APPLYING THE MESSAGE

13. The young ruler's great wealth kept him from fully committing to Jesus. What is your biggest obstacle when it comes to fully committing to Jesus?

_____

_____

_____

_____

14. What evidence in Luke 17–18 do you see that confirms following Christ is the right decision for you?

REFLECTING ON THE MEANING

The story of the healed leper offers several takeaways. The first is the importance of *reflection*. Isolated from society, those who suffered from leprosy had ample opportunity to come to grips with their plight. As they reflected on their prospects for the future, they began to understand how desperately they needed a touch from Almighty God. How often do you reflect on your life? In what areas do you need God to intervene?

The second takeaway is the importance of *response*. Jesus told the lepers to get a certificate of cleansing from the priest *before the cleansing had taken place*. The lepers didn't question Jesus' instructions. They simply obeyed Jesus' words and were healed as they walked to find the priest. In what areas are you struggling to obey God's Word? What might change if you obeyed Him with the kind of faith the lepers showed?

The third takeaway is the importance of *rejoicing*. The leper who came back did more than just offer a polite thank you to Jesus. He glorified God with a loud voice. He fell down on his face at the feet of Jesus. He drew attention to what the Lord had done for him. What can you do to increase the level of rejoicing in your life?

The fourth takeaway is the importance of *returning*. Nine of the lepers set off to immediately enjoy their blessing from the Lord. But the tenth would not take the same approach. Instead, he first returned to properly acknowledge the One who had made it possible. He made the effort to express his gratitude to Christ and was rewarded even more richly for it. What will you do to express your gratitude to Jesus today for His touch in your life?

105

Your blessings may not always be as obvious as the leper's healing, but they are there. If you take the time and effort to identify them—and then return to Christ with your heartfelt prayers of adoration and thanksgiving—you will find that your life is as radically transformed as this man who suffered from leprosy.

JOURNALING YOUR RESPONSE

Keeping the leper's example in mind, how will you show gratitude to Jesus today for something He has accomplished in your life?

ALL ROADS LEAD TO JERUSALEM

Luke 19:1–20:47

GETTING STARTED

What is a situation in your life right now that you are dreading having to face? What steps do you know you need to take to confront that challenge?

_____

_____

_____

_____

_____

_____

_____

_____

_____

_____

_____

_____

_____

_____

_____

_____

_____

SETTING THE STAGE

The Bible contains no descriptions of Jesus laughing or smiling. But that doesn't mean He didn't express happiness or joy. After all, how could He have failed to smile lovingly when the little daughter of Jairus was raised from the dead? How could He have kept from laughing when He was surrounded by children?

The fact is that Jesus experienced a *constant* joy in doing the Lord's work. In Psalm 40:8, we read that He delighted in it. The author of Hebrews states that Jesus, "for the joy that was set before Him endured the cross" (12:2). John wrote that Christ spoke of "My joy" (15:11). Certainly, high and holy feelings of joy and rejoicing were a part of the life of our Lord.

Yet as we read the record of Jesus' ministry, it becomes clear that joy was not the dominant emotion of His life. There seems to be another side that was always present with Him. This came from a realization of the work that He had come to do. It was not happy work from a human perspective. He had come into this world to die. Thus, the Bible refers to Him as "a man of sorrows" who was "acquainted with grief" (Isaiah 53:3).

On at least three occasions, Jesus broke down in tears. According to Hebrews 5:7, He prayed with cries and tears in the Garden of Gethsemane as He contemplated the cross. In John 11:35, He wept along with those who were grieving the death of Lazarus. And in Luke 19:41, Jesus wept over the city of Jerusalem as He predicted its destruction.

EXPLORING THE TEXT

Jesus Comes to Zacchaeus' House (Luke 19:1–10)

---

¹ Then Jesus entered and passed through Jericho. ² Now behold, there was a man named Zacchaeus who was a chief tax collector, and he was rich. ³ And he sought to see who Jesus was, but could not because of the crowd, for he was of short stature. ⁴ So he ran ahead and climbed up into a sycamore tree to see Him, for He was

going to pass that way. ⁵ And when Jesus came to the place, He looked up and saw him, and said to him, "Zacchaeus, make haste and come down, for today I must stay at your house." ⁶ So he made haste and came down, and received Him joyfully. ⁷ But when they saw it, they all complained, saying, "He has gone to be a guest with a man who is a sinner."

⁸ Then Zacchaeus stood and said to the Lord, "Look, Lord, I give half of my goods to the poor; and if I have taken anything from anyone by false accusation, I restore fourfold."

⁹ And Jesus said to him, "Today salvation has come to this house, because he also is a son of Abraham; ¹⁰ for the Son of Man has come to seek and to save that which was lost."

---

1. Who was Zacchaeus? How does Luke describe him? What evidence does this passage provide that Zacchaeus was eager to see Jesus (see verses 1–4)?

_____

_____

_____

_____

_____

2. After Jesus' encounter with the rich young ruler, the disciples had exclaimed, "Who then can be saved?" (Luke 18:26). How did the story of Zacchaeus serve to answer their question (see Luke 19:8–9)?

_____

_____

_____

_____

_____

The Parable of the Minas (Luke 19:11–27)

[11] Now as they heard these things, He spoke another parable, because He was near Jerusalem and because they thought the kingdom of God would appear immediately. [12] Therefore He said: "A certain nobleman went into a far country to receive for himself a kingdom and to return. [13] So he called ten of his servants, delivered to them ten minas, and said to them, 'Do business till I come.' [14] But his citizens hated him, and sent a delegation after him, saying, 'We will not have this man to reign over us.'

[15] "And so it was that when he returned, having received the kingdom, he then commanded these servants, to whom he had given the money, to be called to him, that he might know how much every man had gained by trading. [16] Then came the first, saying, 'Master, your mina has earned ten minas.' [17] And he said to him, 'Well done, good servant; because you were faithful in a very little, have authority over ten cities.' [18] And the second came, saying, 'Master, your mina has earned five minas.' [19] Likewise he said to him, 'You also be over five cities.'

[20] "Then another came, saying, 'Master, here is your mina, which I have kept put away in a handkerchief. [21] For I feared you, because you are an austere man. You collect what you did not deposit, and reap what you did not sow.' [22] And he said to him, 'Out of your own mouth I will judge you, you wicked servant. You knew that I was an austere man, collecting what I did not deposit and reaping what I did not sow. [23] Why then did you not put my money in the bank, that at my coming I might have collected it with interest?'

[24] "And he said to those who stood by, 'Take the mina from him, and give it to him who has ten minas.' [25] (But they said to him, 'Master, he has ten minas.') [26] 'For I say to you, that to everyone who has will be given; and from him who does not have, even what he has will be taken away from him. [27] But bring here those enemies of mine, who did not want me to reign over them, and slay them before me.' "

3. How did the nobleman test his servants' faithfulness? How did he reward the faithfulness of the first two servants (see verses 19:15–19)?

---

4. What were the failures of the third servant? What was the penalty (see verses 20–26)?

The Triumphal Entry (Luke 19:28–48)

²⁸ When He had said this, He went on ahead, going up to Jerusalem. ²⁹ And it came to pass, when He drew near to Bethphage and Bethany, at the mountain called Olivet, that He sent two of His disciples, ³⁰ saying, "Go into the village opposite you, where as you enter you will find a colt tied, on which no one has ever sat. Loose it and bring it here. ³¹ And if anyone asks you, 'Why are you loosing it?' thus you shall say to him, 'Because the Lord has need of it.' "

³² So those who were sent went their way and found it just as He had said to them. ³³ But as they were loosing the colt, the owners of it said to them, "Why are you loosing the colt?"

³⁴ And they said, "The Lord has need of him." ³⁵ Then they brought him to Jesus. And they threw their own clothes on the colt, and they set Jesus on him. ³⁶ And as He went, many spread their clothes on the road.

³⁷ Then, as He was now drawing near the descent of the Mount of Olives, the whole multitude of the disciples began to rejoice and

praise God with a loud voice for all the mighty works they had seen, [38] saying:

" 'Blessed is the King who comes in the name of the Lord!'
Peace in heaven and glory in the highest!"

[39] And some of the Pharisees called to Him from the crowd, "Teacher, rebuke Your disciples."

[40] But He answered and said to them, "I tell you that if these should keep silent, the stones would immediately cry out."

[41] Now as He drew near, He saw the city and wept over it, [42] saying, "If you had known, even you, especially in this your day, the things that make for your peace! But now they are hidden from your eyes. [43] For days will come upon you when your enemies will build an embankment around you, surround you and close you in on every side, [44] and level you, and your children within you, to the ground; and they will not leave in you one stone upon another, because you did not know the time of your visitation."

[45] Then He went into the temple and began to drive out those who bought and sold in it, [46] saying to them, "It is written, 'My house is a house of prayer,' but you have made it a 'den of thieves.' "

[47] And He was teaching daily in the temple. But the chief priests, the scribes, and the leaders of the people sought to destroy Him, [48] and were unable to do anything; for all the people were very attentive to hear Him.

---

5. Read Zechariah 9:9. What do you think the people were expecting as Jesus entered into Jerusalem?

_____

_____

_____

_____

6. Why did Jesus weep as He drew near to Jerusalem? What did He say was going to happen to the city (see verses 41–44)?

_____

_____

_____

_____

_____

The Parable of the Vineyard (Luke 20:9–20)

⁹ Then He began to tell the people this parable: "A certain man planted a vineyard, leased it to vinedressers, and went into a far country for a long time. ¹⁰ Now at vintage-time he sent a servant to the vinedressers, that they might give him some of the fruit of the vineyard. But the vinedressers beat him and sent him away empty-handed. ¹¹ Again he sent another servant; and they beat him also, treated him shamefully, and sent him away empty-handed. ¹² And again he sent a third; and they wounded him also and cast him out.

¹³ "Then the owner of the vineyard said, 'What shall I do? I will send my beloved son. Probably they will respect him when they see him.' ¹⁴ But when the vinedressers saw him, they reasoned among themselves, saying, 'This is the heir. Come, let us kill him, that the inheritance may be ours.' ¹⁵ So they cast him out of the vineyard and killed him. Therefore what will the owner of the vineyard do to them? ¹⁶ He will come and destroy those vinedressers and give the vineyard to others."

And when they heard it they said, "Certainly not!"

¹⁷ Then He looked at them and said, "What then is this that is written:

'The stone which the builders rejected
Has become the chief cornerstone'?

¹⁸ Whoever falls on that stone will be broken; but on whomever it falls, it will grind him to powder."

¹⁹ And the chief priests and the scribes that very hour sought to lay hands on Him, but they feared the people—for they knew He had spoken this parable against them.

²⁰ So they watched Him, and sent spies who pretended to be righteous, that they might seize on His words, in order to deliver Him to the power and the authority of the governor.

---

7. In the parable of the vineyard, the vineyard owner represents God, and the vinedressers represent Israel, the servants represent God's prophets, and the vineyard owner's son represents Jesus. What was Jesus saying about how the people had treated God's prophets? What was Jesus predicting about the treatment He would receive (see verses 9–16)?

_____

_____

_____

_____

_____

_____

8. What did Jesus say would happen to those who rejected His message? How did the chief priests and scribes reveal they understood His point (see verses 17–20)?

_____

_____

_____

_____

_____

_____

REVIEWING THE STORY

Emotions were running high as Jesus made His way to Jerusalem. His enemies were outraged when He first visited the home of the chief tax collector in Jericho. His multitude of followers rejoiced as He approached the city, convinced that He was finally going to lead a rebellion against Rome. But instead of issuing a battle cry, Jesus wept as He drew near Jerusalem. He envisioned the utter destruction of the political and spiritual capital of Israel (a prophecy that would be fulfilled in less than forty years). He spoke of His coming rejection by the people. All the while, the religious leaders continued to plot ways to finally be rid of Him.

9. How does the story of Zacchaeus reveal that Jesus truly came to seek and to save the lost—regardless of that person's past (see Luke 19:1–10)?

_____

_____

_____

_____

_____

_____

_____

10. What are the benefits and challenges of receiving much from God (see Luke 19:11–27)?

_____

_____

_____

_____

_____

_____

_____

11. Why did the Pharisees call out for Jesus to rebuke His followers when He entered into the city? How did Jesus respond to their demands (see Luke 19:39–40)?

_____

_____

_____

_____

_____

_____

12. What was the owner of the vineyard hoping the vinedressers would do when he sent his son to them as an ambassador? Why did the vinedressers kill him (see Luke 20:13–15)?

_____

_____

_____

_____

_____

APPLYING THE MESSAGE

13. Jesus was a guest of Zacchaeus, a despised chief tax collector, and was criticized for regularly spending time with "sinners" (Luke 15:2). With whom do you think Jesus wants you to spend time? How will you do that this week?

_____

_____

_____

_____

_____

14. How are you using the gifts and talents that God has given you to lead others to Christ?

_____

_____

_____

_____

REFLECTING ON THE MEANING

Why did Jesus choose the worst person in town to serve as His host? Why did Jesus spend so much time interacting with tax collectors and the outcasts of society? Luke provides the answer: "The Son of Man has come to seek and to save that which was lost" (19:10). Jesus didn't come to spend time with those who were "good"—with those who saw no need for repentance. Rather, He came to be the ransom for the people who were lost. When the Pharisees questioned Him about His choice of companions, He said, "Those who are well have no need of a physician, but those who are sick" (Luke 5:31).

With His reply, Jesus emphasized to His critics, "I didn't come to be with those who are well. I came to be with those who have a need." We all have a need, but it's not until we _recognize_ our need that we become candidates for salvation. The tax collectors and sinners of Jesus' day didn't have to be persuaded that they needed the Lord. So He sought after them. He came to be the Savior of the world.

Those who seek to please Jesus with their service will follow His lead. For most of us, this means taking a giant leap outside of our comfort zone. It's human nature, after all, to stick with what we know. For many Christians, this involves spending time with Christian friends in Christian settings—and fellowship between believers is certainly an element in our walk with Christ. But Jesus did not intend it to become our primary focus. We are on a search-and-recover mission. Our job is to seek out those who need to hear the good news of Christ—wherever they are—and find the most effective ways to share the good news with them.

JOURNALING YOUR RESPONSE

What percentage of your friends and acquaintances are Christians? Write down your best-guess estimate. What do you think Jesus would say about that percentage?

BEFORE THE ROOSTER CROWS

Luke 21:1–22:71

GETTING STARTED

When was a time that overconfidence got you (or someone you love) in trouble?

_____

_____

_____

_____

_____

_____

_____

_____

_____

_____

SETTING THE STAGE

If you know much about the New Testament, you recognize that to study Peter's early life as a disciple, you have to look into the Gospel narrative, because that is where his story is told. His life after Jesus' resurrection, including his role in the early church, is told in the book of Acts. You also can learn much about him through the two New Testament letters that he wrote. But for the early days, you have to appeal to the Gospels for your information.

One of Peter's great strengths was his outward personality. He was never mistaken for an introvert—in fact, he was an extrovert of the first magnitude. Peter was a natural leader . . . and a strong one. If you had put him in a group of people and asked them a question, nine times out of ten, Peter would have answered for the entire group. He often served as a spokesperson for the disciples, regardless of whether the others wanted him to speak for them. He was just that kind of outgoing, outspoken, confident person.

But as the religious leaders' plots against Jesus began to unfold in Jerusalem, the Lord would test Peter in the area of his strength. Jesus wanted Peter to realize that if he were not careful, he would let down his guard in an area where he assumed he was strong: in his self-assurance and conviction. Peter was thoroughly confident he was ready to stand boldly with Jesus, no matter what came his way. The idea that Satan may have been lying in wait never occurred to him.

Yet when Peter's boldness and confidence were put to the test—no more than a few hours after Jesus' warning—they failed him.

EXPLORING THE TEXT

The Signs of the Times (Luke 21:5–19)

---

5 Then, as some spoke of the temple, how it was adorned with beautiful stones and donations, He said, 6 "These things which you see—the days will come in which not one stone shall be left upon another that shall not be thrown down."

7 So they asked Him, saying, "Teacher, but when will these things be? And what sign will there be when these things are about to take place?"

⁸ And He said: "Take heed that you not be deceived. For many will come in My name, saying, 'I am He,' and, 'The time has drawn near.' Therefore do not go after them. ⁹ But when you hear of wars and commotions, do not be terrified; for these things must come to pass first, but the end will not come immediately."

¹⁰ Then He said to them, "Nation will rise against nation, and kingdom against kingdom. ¹¹ And there will be great earthquakes in various places, and famines and pestilences; and there will be fearful sights and great signs from heaven. ¹² But before all these things, they will lay their hands on you and persecute you, delivering you up to the synagogues and prisons. You will be brought before kings and rulers for My name's sake. ¹³ But it will turn out for you as an occasion for testimony. ¹⁴ Therefore settle it in your hearts not to meditate beforehand on what you will answer; ¹⁵ for I will give you a mouth and wisdom which all your adversaries will not be able to contradict or resist. ¹⁶ You will be betrayed even by parents and brothers, relatives and friends; and they will put some of you to death. ¹⁷ And you will be hated by all for My name's sake. ¹⁸ But not a hair of your head shall be lost. ¹⁹ By your patience possess your souls."

---

1. The temple in Jerusalem was an impressive structure that not only served as the center of Jewish worship but was also a source of Jewish national pride. How did the disciples' comments about the temple reflect these sentiments? How did their words prompt Jesus to reveal what would soon happen to the temple (see verses 5–6)?

_____

_____

_____

_____

_____

2. What warnings about the future did Jesus emphasize to His disciples (see verses 8–19)?

_____

_____

_____

_____

_____

Jesus Institutes the Lord's Supper (Luke 22:1–23)

¹ Now the Feast of Unleavened Bread drew near, which is called Passover. ² And the chief priests and the scribes sought how they might kill Him, for they feared the people.

³ Then Satan entered Judas, surnamed Iscariot, who was numbered among the twelve. ⁴ So he went his way and conferred with the chief priests and captains, how he might betray Him to them. ⁵ And they were glad, and agreed to give him money. ⁶ So he promised and sought opportunity to betray Him to them in the absence of the multitude.

⁷ Then came the Day of Unleavened Bread, when the Passover must be killed. ⁸ And He sent Peter and John, saying, "Go and prepare the Passover for us, that we may eat."

⁹ So they said to Him, "Where do You want us to prepare?"

¹⁰ And He said to them, "Behold, when you have entered the city, a man will meet you carrying a pitcher of water; follow him into the house which he enters. ¹¹ Then you shall say to the master of the house, 'The Teacher says to you, "Where is the guest room where I may eat the Passover with My disciples?" ' ¹² Then he will show you a large, furnished upper room; there make ready."

¹³ So they went and found it just as He had said to them, and they prepared the Passover.

¹⁴ When the hour had come, He sat down, and the twelve apostles with Him. ¹⁵ Then He said to them, "With fervent desire I have desired

to eat this Passover with you before I suffer; [16] for I say to you, I will no longer eat of it until it is fulfilled in the kingdom of God."

[17] Then He took the cup, and gave thanks, and said, "Take this and divide it among yourselves; [18] for I say to you, I will not drink of the fruit of the vine until the kingdom of God comes."

[19] And He took bread, gave thanks and broke it, and gave it to them, saying, "This is My body which is given for you; do this in remembrance of Me."

[20] Likewise He also took the cup after supper, saying, "This cup is the new covenant in My blood, which is shed for you. [21] But behold, the hand of My betrayer is with Me on the table. [22] And truly the Son of Man goes as it has been determined, but woe to that man by whom He is betrayed!"

[23] Then they began to question among themselves, which of them it was who would do this thing.

---

3. How does Luke explain Judas Iscariot's motive for betraying Jesus? What steps did Judas promise to take so the religious leaders could discreetly arrest Jesus (see verses 3–6)?

_____

_____

_____

_____

4. How did Jesus use the symbols of the bread and wine at the Passover meal to remind the disciples in the days and years to come of the significance of His death (see verses 17–22)?

_____

_____

_____

Jesus Predicts Peter's Denial (Luke 22:24–34)

²⁴ Now there was also a dispute among them, as to which of them should be considered the greatest. ²⁵ And He said to them, "The kings of the Gentiles exercise lordship over them, and those who exercise authority over them are called 'benefactors.' ²⁶ But not so among you; on the contrary, he who is greatest among you, let him be as the younger, and he who governs as he who serves.²⁷ For who is greater, he who sits at the table, or he who serves? Is it not he who sits at the table? Yet I am among you as the One who serves.

²⁸ "But you are those who have continued with Me in My trials. ²⁹ And I bestow upon you a kingdom, just as My Father bestowed one upon Me, ³⁰ that you may eat and drink at My table in My kingdom, and sit on thrones judging the twelve tribes of Israel."

³¹ And the Lord said, "Simon, Simon! Indeed, Satan has asked for you, that he may sift you as wheat. ³² But I have prayed for you, that your faith should not fail; and when you have returned to Me, strengthen your brethren."

³³ But he said to Him, "Lord, I am ready to go with You, both to prison and to death."

³⁴ Then He said, "I tell you, Peter, the rooster shall not crow this day before you will deny three times that you know Me."

5. Immediately after Jesus told the disciples that He would be betrayed that night, they began arguing over who should be considered the greatest (see verse 24). What did the disciples obviously still not understand about the events to come?

_____

_____

_____

_____

_____

6. What was Jesus' prayer for Peter? How did Peter respond (see verses 31–33)?

_____

_____

_____

_____

_____

Jesus Arrested in Gethsemane (Luke 22:39–62)

[39] Coming out, He went to the Mount of Olives, as He was accustomed, and His disciples also followed Him. [40] When He came to the place, He said to them, "Pray that you may not enter into temptation."

[41] And He was withdrawn from them about a stone's throw, and He knelt down and prayed, [42] saying, "Father, if it is Your will, take this cup away from Me; nevertheless not My will, but Yours, be done." [43] Then an angel appeared to Him from heaven, strengthening Him. [44] And being in agony, He prayed more earnestly. Then His sweat became like great drops of blood falling down to the ground.

[45] When He rose up from prayer, and had come to His disciples, He found them sleeping from sorrow. [46] Then He said to them, "Why do you sleep? Rise and pray, lest you enter into temptation."

[47] And while He was still speaking, behold, a multitude; and he who was called Judas, one of the twelve, went before them and drew near to Jesus to kiss Him. [48] But Jesus said to him, "Judas, are you betraying the Son of Man with a kiss?"

[49] When those around Him saw what was going to happen, they said to Him, "Lord, shall we strike with the sword?" [50] And one of them struck the servant of the high priest and cut off his right ear.

[51] But Jesus answered and said, "Permit even this." And He touched his ear and healed him.

[52] Then Jesus said to the chief priests, captains of the temple, and the elders who had come to Him, "Have you come out, as against

a robber, with swords and clubs? ⁵³ When I was with you daily in the temple, you did not try to seize Me. But this is your hour, and the power of darkness."

⁵⁴ Having arrested Him, they led Him and brought Him into the high priest's house. But Peter followed at a distance. ⁵⁵ Now when they had kindled a fire in the midst of the courtyard and sat down together, Peter sat among them. ⁵⁶ And a certain servant girl, seeing him as he sat by the fire, looked intently at him and said, "This man was also with Him."

⁵⁷ But he denied Him, saying, "Woman, I do not know Him."

⁵⁸ And after a little while another saw him and said, "You also are of them."

But Peter said, "Man, I am not!"

⁵⁹ Then after about an hour had passed, another confidently affirmed, saying, "Surely this fellow also was with Him, for he is a Galilean."

⁶⁰ But Peter said, "Man, I do not know what you are saying!"

Immediately, while he was still speaking, the rooster crowed. ⁶¹ And the Lord turned and looked at Peter. Then Peter remembered the word of the Lord, how He had said to him, "Before the rooster crows, you will deny Me three times." ⁶² So Peter went out and wept bitterly.

---

7. What does this story reveal about Jesus' state of mind as He prayed in the Garden of Gethsemane? How did God affirm that Jesus was doing His will (see verses 42–44)?

8. John's Gospel reveals that it was Peter who cut off the right ear of the servant of the high priest (see John 18:10). How did Peter follow up this act of boldness (see Luke 22:54–60)?

_____

_____

_____

_____

REVIEWING THE STORY

Circumstances deteriorated rapidly after Jesus and His followers arrived in Jerusalem. Jesus didn't sugarcoat the situation. He warned His disciples they would soon face intense persecution and that most would follow Him in death. Peter tried to play the hero, but Jesus set him straight. Jesus' arrest a few hours later shook Peter and the other disciples to the core. Peter put up a token defense with a sword, but Jesus stopped him. The disciples couldn't see God's plan unfolding. Through it all, however, Jesus gave them hope and promises to which they could cling.

9. Jesus shared a dire prediction with His disciples about the fate of the temple. What promises did Jesus also offer (see Luke 21:10–19)?

_____

_____

_____

_____

10. Why was Jesus so adamant about eating the Passover meal in Jerusalem with His disciples (see Luke 22:14–18)?

_____

_____

_____

_____

11. What did Jesus say that Satan wanted to do to Peter (see Luke 22:31–32)?

_____

_____

_____

_____

_____

12. Aside from the agony and dread that Jesus felt about His impending crucifixion, what other concerns may have been weighing heavily on Jesus' heart as He prayed in the Garden of Gethsemane (see Luke 22:39–46)?

_____

_____

_____

_____

_____

APPLYING THE MESSAGE

13. In what situations are you tempted to deny Jesus or downplay your relationship with Him?

_____

_____

_____

_____

_____

14. Jesus prayed that Peter's faith would not fail and that he would strengthen the other disciples. Who are some people you know who need to be encouraged in their faith?

_____

_____

_____

_____

_____

REFLECTING ON THE MEANING

Peter's self-confidence was a sign of his self-ignorance. In fact, all self-confidence, apart from Christ, is an indication of ignorance. As stated in Proverbs 28:26, "He who trusts in his own heart is a fool." Why? Because "the heart is deceitful above all things, and desperately wicked" (Jeremiah 17:9). If you put all of your trust in yourself, you're going to discover that you have trusted in someone who is not trustworthy.

This is not to say there's anything wrong with a person being confident. Confidence is a necessary part of life. In sports, people say that when you lose your confidence, you can't play. When you lose the confidence that you _can_ perform, you lose your ability _to_ perform. So there's nothing wrong with being confident in who you are.

But the people who have the greatest sense of confidence are those who are rightly related to Jesus, who are in the center of God's will, and who are asking God by His Spirit to fill them every day. These people can walk with their shoulders back, their heads held high, and a spring in their step, knowing they're doing what God wants them to be doing. They can go forward to be the people God has called them to be and never hide their spiritual identities.

The temptation to place too much trust in yourself can be overwhelming. Entire advertising campaigns are built around the concept of letting "you be you"—thus being answerable to no one else when it comes to your identity, your potential, and your place of importance in the world. You can avoid all kinds of pitfalls and hard lessons by surrendering your self-confidence to God and exchanging it for genuine confidence through Him.

JOURNALING YOUR RESPONSE

How can you tell if your confidence is in yourself or in God?

CRUCIFIXION AND RESURRECTION

Luke 23:1–24:53

GETTING STARTED

When was a time you were accused of something you didn't do? How did you respond?

_____

_____

_____

_____

_____

_____

_____

_____

_____

_____

_____

_____

_____

_____

_____

_____

_____

_____

SETTING THE STAGE

When Jesus came out of the grave on the first Easter morning, He came into a world that was troubled. It was a world where the Jewish people had long been under the heel of Roman domination . . . a yoke they sought desperately to throw off. Jesus came into a world where five million people (conservatively) were slaves with cruel masters. He came into a world where the infant mortality rate was very high, with many children dying before the age of six. Plagues swept unchecked throughout that world. Taxation was a tremendous burden.

People who lived during that time were men and women who wept and worried. Among them were the friends of Jesus. After His crucifixion, the followers who had watched Him perform miracles were in shock. Two men were sorrowful as they walked on the road to Emmaus. Eleven of His disciples were confused and disillusioned as they gathered behind closed doors to wonder and to wait. No one knew what would happen next.

Mary Magdalene and the other women who came to minister to the Lord were overwhelmed with sorrow and hopelessness. They were bringing spices to anoint the dead body of their anticipated Messiah because they believed it was all over . . . for Him and for them. They loved Him with a great love and wanted to honor Him even in His death. Jesus had told them of His resurrection, but they had not believed Him or understood Him. The angels at the tomb had to remind the women of Jesus' words.

This is how it was on that first Easter morning. Love was alive in the hearts of these women who came to minister to Jesus, but faith and hope lay crushed within His grave.

EXPLORING THE TEXT

Jesus Before Pilate and Herod (Luke 23:1–25)

---

¹ Then the whole multitude of them arose and led Him to Pilate. ² And they began to accuse Him, saying, "We found this fellow perverting

the nation, and forbidding to pay taxes to Caesar, saying that He Himself is Christ, a King."

³ Then Pilate asked Him, saying, "Are You the King of the Jews?"

He answered him and said, "It is as you say."

⁴ So Pilate said to the chief priests and the crowd, "I find no fault in this Man."

⁵ But they were the more fierce, saying, "He stirs up the people, teaching throughout all Judea, beginning from Galilee to this place."

⁶ When Pilate heard of Galilee, he asked if the Man were a Galilean. ⁷ And as soon as he knew that He belonged to Herod's jurisdiction, he sent Him to Herod, who was also in Jerusalem at that time. ⁸ Now when Herod saw Jesus, he was exceedingly glad; for he had desired for a long time to see Him, because he had heard many things about Him, and he hoped to see some miracle done by Him. ⁹ Then he questioned Him with many words, but He answered him nothing. ¹⁰ And the chief priests and scribes stood and vehemently accused Him. ¹¹ Then Herod, with his men of war, treated Him with contempt and mocked Him, arrayed Him in a gorgeous robe, and sent Him back to Pilate. ¹² That very day Pilate and Herod became friends with each other, for previously they had been at enmity with each other.

¹³ Then Pilate, when he had called together the chief priests, the rulers, and the people, ¹⁴ said to them, "You have brought this Man to me, as one who misleads the people. And indeed, having examined Him in your presence, I have found no fault in this Man concerning those things of which you accuse Him; ¹⁵ no, neither did Herod, for I sent you back to him; and indeed nothing deserving of death has been done by Him. ¹⁶ I will therefore chastise Him and release Him" ¹⁷ (for it was necessary for him to release one to them at the feast).

¹⁸ And they all cried out at once, saying, "Away with this Man, and release to us Barabbas"— ¹⁹ who had been thrown into prison for a certain rebellion made in the city, and for murder.

²⁰ Pilate, therefore, wishing to release Jesus, again called out to them. ²¹ But they shouted, saying, "Crucify Him, crucify Him!"

²² Then he said to them the third time, "Why, what evil has He done? I have found no reason for death in Him. I will therefore chastise Him and let Him go."

²³ But they were insistent, demanding with loud voices that He be crucified. And the voices of these men and of the chief priests prevailed. ²⁴ So Pilate gave sentence that it should be as they requested. ²⁵ And he released to them the one they requested, who for rebellion and murder had been thrown into prison; but he delivered Jesus to their will.

---

1. What tactics did Pilate employ to try to avoid the responsibility of sentencing Jesus to death (see verses 6–8, 13–17)?

_____

_____

_____

_____

_____

_____

2. Why do you think Pilate eventually relented and agreed to free the criminal Barabbas instead of Jesus (see verses 20–23)?

_____

_____

_____

_____

_____

_____

_____

The King on a Cross (Luke 23:26–46)

²⁶ Now as they led Him away, they laid hold of a certain man, Simon a Cyrenian, who was coming from the country, and on him they laid the cross that he might bear it after Jesus.

²⁷ And a great multitude of the people followed Him, and women who also mourned and lamented Him. ²⁸ But Jesus, turning to them, said, "Daughters of Jerusalem, do not weep for Me, but weep for yourselves and for your children. ²⁹ For indeed the days are coming in which they will say, 'Blessed are the barren, wombs that never bore, and breasts which never nursed!' ³⁰ Then they will begin 'to say to the mountains, "Fall on us!" and to the hills, "Cover us!" ' ³¹ For if they do these things in the green wood, what will be done in the dry?"

³² There were also two others, criminals, led with Him to be put to death. ³³ And when they had come to the place called Calvary, there they crucified Him, and the criminals, one on the right hand and the other on the left. ³⁴ Then Jesus said, "Father, forgive them, for they do not know what they do."

And they divided His garments and cast lots. ³⁵ And the people stood looking on. But even the rulers with them sneered, saying, "He saved others; let Him save Himself if He is the Christ, the chosen of God."

³⁶ The soldiers also mocked Him, coming and offering Him sour wine, ³⁷ and saying, "If You are the King of the Jews, save Yourself."

³⁸ And an inscription also was written over Him in letters of Greek, Latin, and Hebrew:

THIS IS THE KING OF THE JEWS.

³⁹ Then one of the criminals who were hanged blasphemed Him, saying, "If You are the Christ, save Yourself and us."

⁴⁰ But the other, answering, rebuked him, saying, "Do you not even fear God, seeing you are under the same condemnation? ⁴¹ And

we indeed justly, for we receive the due reward of our deeds; but this Man has done nothing wrong." ⁴²Then he said to Jesus, "Lord, remember me when You come into Your kingdom."

⁴³And Jesus said to him, "Assuredly, I say to you, today you will be with Me in Paradise."

⁴⁴Now it was about the sixth hour, and there was darkness over all the earth until the ninth hour. ⁴⁵Then the sun was darkened, and the veil of the temple was torn in two. ⁴⁶And when Jesus had cried out with a loud voice, He said, "Father, 'into Your hands I commit My spirit.' " Having said this, He breathed His last.

---

3. How was Jesus' crucifixion made even *more* agonizing by the people who witnessed it (see verses 35–39)?

_____

_____

_____

_____

_____

_____

4. One of the criminals hanging next to Jesus recognized that He had done nothing wrong. What did this criminal recognize about his own condition? How did Jesus respond to him (see verses 40–43)?

_____

_____

_____

_____

_____

_____

Jesus Is Risen (Luke 24:1–27)

[1] Now on the first day of the week, very early in the morning, they, and certain other women with them, came to the tomb bringing the spices which they had prepared. [2] But they found the stone rolled away from the tomb. [3] Then they went in and did not find the body of the Lord Jesus. [4] And it happened, as they were greatly perplexed about this, that behold, two men stood by them in shining garments. [5] Then, as they were afraid and bowed their faces to the earth, they said to them, "Why do you seek the living among the dead? [6] He is not here, but is risen! Remember how He spoke to you when He was still in Galilee, [7] saying, 'The Son of Man must be delivered into the hands of sinful men, and be crucified, and the third day rise again.' "

[8] And they remembered His words. [9] Then they returned from the tomb and told all these things to the eleven and to all the rest. [10] It was Mary Magdalene, Joanna, Mary the mother of James, and the other women with them, who told these things to the apostles. [11] And their words seemed to them like idle tales, and they did not believe them. [12] But Peter arose and ran to the tomb; and stooping down, he saw the linen cloths lying by themselves; and he departed, marveling to himself at what had happened.

[13] Now behold, two of them were traveling that same day to a village called Emmaus, which was seven miles from Jerusalem. [14] And they talked together of all these things which had happened. [15] So it was, while they conversed and reasoned, that Jesus Himself drew near and went with them. [16] But their eyes were restrained, so that they did not know Him.

[17] And He said to them, "What kind of conversation is this that you have with one another as you walk and are sad?"

[18] Then the one whose name was Cleopas answered and said to Him, "Are You the only stranger in Jerusalem, and have You not known the things which happened there in these days?"

[19] And He said to them, "What things?"

So they said to Him, "The things concerning Jesus of Nazareth, who was a Prophet mighty in deed and word before God and all the people, [20] and how the chief priests and our rulers delivered Him to be condemned to death, and crucified Him. [21] But we were hoping that it was He who was going to redeem Israel. Indeed, besides all this, today is the third day since these things happened. [22] Yes, and certain women of our company, who arrived at the tomb early, astonished us. [23] When they did not find His body, they came saying that they had also seen a vision of angels who said He was alive. [24] And certain of those who were with us went to the tomb and found it just as the women had said; but Him they did not see."

[25] Then He said to them, "O foolish ones, and slow of heart to believe in all that the prophets have spoken! [26] Ought not the Christ to have suffered these things and to enter into His glory?" [27] And beginning at Moses and all the Prophets, He expounded to them in all the Scriptures the things concerning Himself.

---

5. How did the disciples react to the women's news that Jesus had risen from the dead (see verses 11–12)?

_____

_____

_____

_____

6. How did Jesus respond to the two men traveling on the road to Emmaus who were trying to come to grips with His death (see verses 25–27)?

_____

_____

_____

_____

Jesus Appears to the Disciples (Luke 24:28–48)

[28] Then they drew near to the village where they were going, and He indicated that He would have gone farther. [29] But they constrained Him, saying, "Abide with us, for it is toward evening, and the day is far spent." And He went in to stay with them.

[30] Now it came to pass, as He sat at the table with them, that He took bread, blessed and broke it, and gave it to them. [31] Then their eyes were opened and they knew Him; and He vanished from their sight.

[32] And they said to one another, "Did not our heart burn within us while He talked with us on the road, and while He opened the Scriptures to us?" [33] So they rose up that very hour and returned to Jerusalem, and found the eleven and those who were with them gathered together, [34] saying, "The Lord is risen indeed, and has appeared to Simon!" [35] And they told about the things that had happened on the road, and how He was known to them in the breaking of bread.

[36] Now as they said these things, Jesus Himself stood in the midst of them, and said to them, "Peace to you." [37] But they were terrified and frightened, and supposed they had seen a spirit. [38] And He said to them, "Why are you troubled? And why do doubts arise in your hearts? [39] Behold My hands and My feet, that it is I Myself. Handle Me and see, for a spirit does not have flesh and bones as you see I have."

[40] When He had said this, He showed them His hands and His feet. [41] But while they still did not believe for joy, and marveled, He said to them, "Have you any food here?" [42] So they gave Him a piece of a broiled fish and some honeycomb. [43] And He took it and ate in their presence.

[44] Then He said to them, "These are the words which I spoke to you while I was still with you, that all things must be fulfilled which were written in the Law of Moses and the Prophets and the Psalms concerning Me." [45] And He opened their understanding, that they might comprehend the Scriptures.

⁴⁶ Then He said to them, "Thus it is written, and thus it was necessary for the Christ to suffer and to rise from the dead the third day, ⁴⁷ and that repentance and remission of sins should be preached in His name to all nations, beginning at Jerusalem. ⁴⁸ And you are witnesses of these things."

---

7. What impact did Jesus' words have on the two men (see verses 28–35)?

_____

_____

_____

_____

_____

_____

_____

_____

_____

_____

8. What did Jesus do to calm the disciples of their fear (see verses 36–48)?

_____

_____

_____

_____

_____

_____

_____

_____

_____

_____

REVIEWING THE STORY

There was nothing fair or just about Jesus' trial and execution. He was innocent not only of all the charges leveled against Him but also of any wrongdoing whatsoever. He was blameless. The darkness that fell while Jesus hung on the cross ultimately served to silence those who had accused and taunted Him. A centurion who witnessed His death spoke the truth when he said, "Certainly this was a righteous Man!" (Luke 23:47). But Jesus' death on the cross was not the end of the story. A group of female followers were the first ones to discover that Jesus had risen from the grave. Then the astonishing news spread when Jesus opened the eyes of two men on the road to Emmaus. Then the astonishing news spread to the rest of His disciples as well when He appeared to them in the flesh . . . and shared a meal with them.

9. What conclusion did Pilate and Herod both reach after they heard the charges against Jesus (see Luke 23:6–17)?

_____

_____

_____

_____

_____

_____

10. How did Jesus demonstrate His love for the people of Israel even as He was being led away to the cross (see Luke 23:27–34)?

_____

_____

_____

_____

_____

11. Look at Luke 24:9–12 and John 20:24–29. How was Peter's reaction to the news of Jesus' resurrection similar to and different from Thomas' reaction?

_____

_____

_____

_____

_____

_____

12. What did Jesus say to help His disciples understand the events of the previous three days (see Luke 24:44–48)?

_____

_____

_____

_____

_____

_____

APPLYING THE MESSAGE

13. The criminal who hung next to Jesus received salvation when he called out to Christ. What does this tell you about God's grace—and how God responds to those who trust Him?

_____

_____

_____

_____

_____

14. Jesus opened the two disciples' eyes on the road to Emmaus and revealed how He was the Messiah promised in Scripture. How has Jesus opened your eyes to this fact as well?

_____

_____

_____

_____

REFLECTING ON THE MEANING

The resurrection of Jesus changed the world. More importantly, it changed _lives_. The women at the tomb were changed. They came to Jesus' burial site downcast and forlorn, but they raced back excitedly to tell the others what they had found. The eleven disciples who had been cowering in a room became bold and fearless. They would end up risking their very lives to preach the gospel . . . because the resurrection had changed everything for them.

When people come to know the risen Christ, it transforms the world in which they live. When a plague broke out in AD 250—killing as many as 5,000 people each day in the city of Rome—the Christians stayed behind to tend to the sick while others fled. The news about the Christians spread, and a few decades later, in AD 306, the Emperor Constantine came to power and declared religious tolerance for Christians throughout the Roman Empire. Christians were later instrumental in getting the popular but cruel gladiatorial contests banned in Rome.

The resurrection of Jesus Christ continues to change the lives of those who are exposed to it. Given the proper consideration, it can become the most exciting event in a person's life. The resurrection of Jesus is the _essence_ of hope, for the power with which Jesus conquered the grave is available to all who believe in Him. This power blurs the lines between what is possible and what is impossible. Thus, the resurrection of Jesus is hope for the drug addict and the person dominated by alcohol. It is hope for the troubled marriage and the person filled with hate. It is hope for the person struggling with physical, emotional, or mental health. It is hope for the grieving parent, spouse, child, and friend.

Jesus Christ, the resurrected Lord, is *hope*. And just as he changed the lives of the people in that troubled world when Easter first dawned, He continues to change the lives of people today.

JOURNALING YOUR RESPONSE

In what area of your life do you most need the hope of Jesus' resurrection?

LEADER'S GUIDE

Thank you for choosing to lead your group through this study from Dr. David Jeremiah on *The Gospel of Luke*. Being a group leader has its own rewards, and it is our prayer that your walk with the Lord will deepen through this experience. During the twelve lessons in this study, you and your group will read selected passages from Luke, explore key themes in the Gospel based on teachings from Dr. Jeremiah, and review questions that will encourage group discussion. There are multiple components in this section that can help you structure your lessons and discussion time, so please be sure to read and consider each one.

BEFORE YOU BEGIN

Before your first meeting, make sure you and your group are well-versed with the content of the lesson. Group members should have their own copy of *The Gospel of Luke* study guide prior to the first meeting so they can follow along and record their answers, thoughts, and insights. After the first week, you may wish to assign the study guide lesson as homework prior to the group meeting and then use the meeting time to discuss the content in the lesson.

To ensure everyone has a chance to participate in the discussion, the ideal size for a group is around eight to ten people. If there are more than ten people, break up the bigger group into smaller subgroups. Make sure the members are committed to participating each week, as this will help create stability and help you better prepare the structure of the meeting.

At the beginning of each week's study, start with the opening Getting Started question to introduce the topic you will be discussing. The members should answer briefly, as the goal is just for them to have an idea of the subject in their minds as you go over the lesson. This will allow the members to become engaged and ready to interact with the rest of the group.

After reviewing the lesson, try to initiate a free-flowing discussion. Invite group members to bring questions and insights they may have discovered to the next meeting, especially if they were unsure of the meaning of some parts of the lesson. Be prepared to discuss how biblical truth applies to the world we live in today.

Weekly Preparation

As the group leader, here are a few things you can do to prepare for each meeting:

- *Be thoroughly familiar with the material in the lesson.* Make sure you understand the content of each lesson so you know how to structure the group time and are prepared to lead the group discussion.

- *Decide, ahead of time, which questions you want to discuss.* Depending on how much time you have each week, you may not be able to reflect on every question. Select specific questions that you feel will evoke the best discussion.

- *Take prayer requests.* At the end of your discussion, take prayer requests from your group members and then pray for one another.

Structuring the Discussion Time

There are several ways to structure the duration of the study. You can choose to cover each lesson individually, for a total of twelve weeks of group meetings, or you can combine two lessons together per week, for a total of six weeks of group meetings. You can also have the group members read just the selected passages of Scripture that are given in each lesson, or they can cover the entire Gospel of Luke. The following charts illustrates these options:

TWELVE-WEEK FORMAT

Week	Lessons Covered	Expanded Reading
1	God with Us	*Luke 1:1–2:52*
2	Baptism and Temptation	*Luke 3:1–4:44*
3	Four Men and a Savior	*Luke 5:1–6:49*
4	People Are Important	*Luke 7:1–8:56*
5	Who Is My Neighbor?	*Luke 9:1–10:42*
6	A Master Class in Prayer	*Luke 11:1–12:59*
7	Count the Cost	*Luke 13:1–14:35*
8	Lost and Found	*Luke 15:1–16:31*
9	Encounters with Jesus	*Luke 17:1–18:43*
10	All Roads Lead to Jerusalem	*Luke 19:1–20:47*
11	Before the Rooster Crows	*Luke 21:1–22:71*
12	Crucifixion and Resurrection	*Luke 23:1–24:53*

SIX-WEEK FORMAT

Week	Lessons Covered	Expanded Reading
1	God with Us / Baptism and Temptation	*Luke 1:1–4:44*
2	Four Men and a Savior / People Are Important	*Luke 5:1–8:56*
3	Who Is My Neighbor? / A Master Class in Prayer	*Luke 9:1–12:59*
4	Count the Cost / Lost and Found	*Luke 13:1–16:31*
5	Encounters with Jesus / All Roads Lead to Jerusalem	*Luke 17:1–20:47*
6	Before the Rooster Crows / Crucifixion and Resurrection	*Luke 21:1–24:53*

In regard to organizing your time when planning your group Bible study, the following two schedules, for sixty minutes and ninety minutes, can give you a structure for the lesson:

Section	60 Minutes	90 Minutes
Welcome: Members arrive and get settled	5 minutes	10 minutes
Getting Started Question: Prepares the group for interacting with one another	10 minutes	10 minutes
Message: Review the lesson	15 minutes	25 minutes
Discussion: Discuss questions in the lesson	25 minutes	35 minutes
Review and Prayer: Review the key points of the lesson and have a closing time of prayer	5 minutes	10 minutes

As the group leader, it is up to you to keep track of the time and keep things moving according to your schedule. If your group is having a good discussion, don't feel the need to stop and move on to the next question. Remember, the purpose is to pull together ideas and share unique insights on the lesson. Encourage everyone to participate, but don't be concerned if certain group members are more quiet. They may just be internally reflecting on the questions and need time to process their ideas before they can share them.

GROUP DYNAMICS

Leading a group study can be a rewarding experience for you and your group members—but that doesn't mean there won't be challenges. Certain members may feel uncomfortable discussing topics that they consider very personal and might be afraid of being called on. Some members might have disagreements on specific issues. To help prevent these scenarios, consider the following ground rules:

- If someone has a question that may seem off topic, suggest that it is discussed at another time, or ask the group if they are okay with addressing that topic.

- If someone asks a question you don't know the answer to, confess that you don't know and move on. If you feel comfortable, invite other group members to give their opinions or share their comments based on personal experience.
- If you feel like a couple of people are talking much more than others, direct questions to people who may not have shared yet. You could even ask the more dominating members to help draw out the quiet ones.
- When there is a disagreement, encourage the group members to process the matter in love. Invite members from opposing sides to evaluate their opinions and consider the ideas of the other members. Lead the group through Scripture that addresses the topic, and look for common ground.

When issues arise, encourage your group to think of Scripture: "Love one another" (John 13:34), "If it is possible, as much as it depends on you, live peaceably with all men" (Romans 12:18), and, "Be swift to hear, slow to speak, slow to wrath" (James 1:19).

ABOUT
Dr. David Jeremiah and Turning Point

Dr. David Jeremiah is the founder of Turning Point, a ministry committed to providing Christians with sound Bible teaching relevant to today's changing times through radio and television broadcasts, audio series, books, and live events. Dr. Jeremiah's teaching on topics such as family, prayer, worship, angels, and biblical prophecy forms the foundation of Turning Point.

David and his wife, Donna, reside in El Cajon, California, where he serves as the senior pastor of Shadow Mountain Community Church. David and Donna have four children and twelve grandchildren.

In 1982, Dr. Jeremiah brought the same solid teaching to San Diego television that he shares weekly with his congregation. Shortly thereafter, Turning Point expanded its ministry to radio. Dr. Jeremiah's inspiring messages can now be heard worldwide on radio, television, and the internet.

Because Dr. Jeremiah desires to know his listening audience, he travels nationwide holding ministry rallies and spiritual enrichment conferences that touch the hearts and lives of many people. According to Dr. Jeremiah, "At some point in time, everyone reaches a turning point; and for every person, that moment is unique, an experience to hold onto forever. There's so much changing in today's world that sometimes it's difficult to choose the right path. Turning Point offers people an understanding of God's Word and seeks to make a difference in their lives."

Dr. Jeremiah has authored numerous books, including *Escape the Coming Night* (Revelation), *The Handwriting on the Wall* (Daniel), *Overcoming Loneliness*, *Prayer—The Great Adventure*, *God in You* (Holy Spirit), *When*

Your World Falls Apart, Slaying the Giants in Your Life, My Heart's Desire, Hope for Today, Captured by Grace, Signs of Life, What in the World Is Going On?, The Coming Economic Armageddon, I Never Thought I'd See the Day!, God Loves You: He Always Has—He Always Will, Agents of the Apocalypse, Agents of Babylon, Revealing the Mysteries of Heaven, People Are Asking . . . Is This the End?, A Life Beyond Amazing, Overcomer, and *The Book of Signs.*

STAY CONNECTED
to Dr. David Jeremiah

Take advantage of two great ways to let Dr. David Jeremiah give you spiritual direction every day!

Turning Points Magazine and Devotional

Receive Dr. David Jeremiah's magazine, *Turning Points*, each month and discover:

- Thematic study focus
- 48 pages of life-changing reading
- Relevant articles
- Special features
- Daily devotional readings
- Bible study resource offers
- Live event schedule
- Radio & television information

Request *Turning Points* magazine today!

(800) 947-1993
www.DavidJeremiah.org/Magazine

Daily Turning Point E-Devotional

Start your day off right! Find words of inspiration and spiritual motivation waiting for you on your computer every morning! Receive a daily e-devotion communication from David Jeremiah that will strengthen your walk with God and encourage you to live the authentic Christian life.

Request your free e-devotional today!

(800) 947-1993
www.DavidJeremiah.org/Devo